29

臺北帝國大學研究年報 第廿九冊

林慶彰 總策畫
民國時期稀見期刊彙編
第一輯

文學科研究年報
言語と文學③④

# 文學科研究年報

言語と文學

第三輯

臺北帝國大學文政學部

# はしがき

## はしがき

　この草稿が最初に書かれたのはもはや四・五年前のことである。今これを筐底から取りだして筆を加へてみても、容易に筆者現在の氣持に近づかうとはしない。もしも自己に忠實であらうとするならば、おそらく單なる補筆ではなく、全然初めから書き直すことが必要なのであらう。しかし筆者には今そのやうな時間の餘裕もないし、新しい心境は古い題目の再吟味よりは新しい題目の新しい取扱ひに向つてゐる。されば筆者は今この草稿を發表するにあたり　それが筆者の現在を表示するものとしてではなく、過去の一時期を記念するものとして受けとられることを希望する。

　なほこの試論はサブタイトルにことわつてあるやうに、主としてサミュエル・バトラーの思想と藝術をとりあつかつたものである。從つて彼の生涯に關する記述は省略されてゐるが、もしそのやうなものを要求する讀者があ

## はしがき

つたら 終りの年譜を一種の代用物として参照されたい。また書誌はバトラーをさらにより詳しく研究しようとする人々のために多少でも参考になれば幸である。

# 目次

はしがき……………………………………………一

一 ヴィクトリアニズム……………………………一

二 諷刺………………………………………………三

三 科學………………………………………………三

四 「萬人の道」……………………………………五

五 晩年の諸作………………………………………公

年譜…………………………………………………六

書誌…………………………………………………一〇五

# ヴィクトリアニズム

現在の人と文學は進んで時代に適應しようとする場合には勿論のこと、反對に昔時代から遁れようとする場合にもかく努力することに於てかへつてその時代の性格を持ち、實際なんらかの性格を持つのでなければ、人と人との文學は時代の名によつて呼ばれる資格がないのであらう。そしてこのやうな性格に就いて現代の文學を考へるとき、その文學からは、現代に住めるしかし新しい時代の精神の稀薄な、多くの作家が後景におしやられるとともに、年代的には過去に屬する、しかし精神に於ては新しい、少數の作家が、介在する時間をおしのけて視野の前景にあらはれ、我々の注意と考慮を要求する。サミュエル・バトラー(Samuel Butler, 1835–1902)はこのやうな少數の作家の一人である。

## 一 ヴィクトリアニズム

バトラーの現代に對する意義は消極と積極との二つの方面から考へられ

## 一　ヴィクトリアニズム

　消極的には彼は十九世紀、特にヴィクトリアニズムの否定者であり、かく過去を否定することによつて彼は現代を可能にした批評家の一人であるといふことができる。積極的には彼は人間と社會とに對する新しい態度、特にリアリズムの精神を提示したことによつて、直接現代の作家に接合する。そしてこれら二つのもの——批評とリアリズム、過去の否定と新しい時代の創造——はバトラーに於て別々にあるのではなく、前者は後者のうちに入りこみ、後者は前者によつて用意されてゐるのである。
　ヴィクトリアニズム (Victorianism) は今日殆んど全く「時代遅れ」の同意語に轉化したやうにみえる。それは非難と嘲笑との對象にされ、或は屢〻 "good old times" としてなつかしまれるほども遠く切り離された、無害な過去のやうに考へられてゐる。ヴィクトリア朝の文學は、小説に於てはディッケンズやサッカレイ、詩に於てはテニスンやブラウニング、批評に於てはカーライルやラスキンを含んでゐるにもかゝはらず、それらの偉大な名前も落目（おちめ）になつた時代の名譽を救ふことができず、時にはそれらの名前そのものがアイロ

## 一　ヴィクトリアニズム

十九世紀のイギリスは、華やかなロマンティシズムにもかゝはらず、最初からその出發に或る全く正常でないものがあつた。十九世紀のイギリスは、フランス革命から始まつたといふよりもフランスで始まつたといふよりもフランスで始まつたといふよりもフランスで始まつたといふよりもフランスで始まつたといふよりもフランスで始まつたといふよりもフランスで始まつた

ニーの對象になつてゐる。それはあたかも年とつた巨人の末路のやうに、それが巨大であつたゞけ、かへつてその沒落がめざましく、沒落の悲劇のうちに或るぶざまなもの、殆んど喜劇的なものが入りこんでゐる。そして 'philistinism'（俗物根性）、'snobbery'（同じく俗物根性）、見かけ倒しの 'respectability'（世間體）、趣味に於ける低俗と精神の空虛――これらのものが最近三十年間にヴィクトリアニズムの符牒として一般の心に印象されたものである。しかしあんなにも堂々とした外觀を持ち、單なる存續の長さから言つても歷史上比類の少いヴィクトリアニズムが、何故あのやうに脆く崩壞し、單なる空虛となり、空虛以上に積極的な虛僞となつたのであらうか。それは如何なる理由により、如何なる經過をたどつて起つたのであらうか。またその空虛或は虛僞の質或は內容は如何なるものであらうか。

# 一 ヴィクトリアニズム

といふ方が適當である――ちやうど世紀末の英文學が、その或る樣相に於ては、同じフランスで終つたやうに。フランス革命は、言ふまでもなく、中産市民階級の政治運動であつた。しかし産業革命のより進んだ段階にあつたイギリスに於ては、それが經濟的に進んでゐたといふ、ちやうどその理由で、このやうな政治革命は起らず、政治形體は經濟組織の後から進んで、時とともに自己をこれに適應せしめた。しかし

When France in wrath her giant-limbs upreared,
And with that oath, which smote air, earth, and sea,
Stamped her strong foot and said she would be free,

(S. T. Coleridge, *France, an Ode*)

フランスが怒つて巨人のやうな足をあげ、
　空と、大地と、海を打つ叫びをもつて
　足ぶみしつゝ、われは自由を欲すと言ひし時、
イギリスの若者たちが歡呼してこれを迎へ、彼等自身の國にもかくの如き

## 一 ヴィクトリアニズム

一大變動が來ることを豫想したのは當然であつた。ワーヅワス、コウルリッヂからバイロン、シェリーにいたる若いロマンティシストたちの詩には、このやうな豫想と期待が虹のやうにかゝつてゐる。しかしその希望がすべての虹のやうに求めればしりぞき、近づけば消えて行つたとき、實際の世界に於て阻まれた若い詩人たちの熱情は空想と觀念とのうちに出口を求めた。そしてそこに現實にはなき理想の國を描かうと、或は純粹な心情のアラベスクをひろげようと、いづれにしてもロマンティックな詩歌は實際の革命に對する代用物であつた。それゆゑにイギリスのロマンティシズムにはフランスに見られぬ強い反抗と狂亂の精神があつた。同じ原因から、同時にしかしながら、そこには現實からの遊離、實際的な無力と無效果、觀念そのものの狹さと偏り、心情の或るもの思はしい蔭があつた。この蔭は彼等の理想と現實との距離が大きくなり、彼等が言はゞ實際の世界に於ける流謫の人であることを自覺するに從つて、次第に積極的な憂ひと悲しみに深まつていつた。

# 一 ヴィクトリアニズム

そしてまたロマンティシストたちは歴史的、社會的に一つの中間的、過渡的な存在であった。彼等はその思想と情操とに於て貴族的な多くのものを持ち、新興社會層としての中産市民階級よりも、沒落し或は變質してゆく貴族の過去に心をひかれた。彼等は實際的でなく空想的であったやうに、進步的といふよりはむしろ懷古的であった。當時古い貴族階級は次第にブルジョア化し、新しいブルジョアはまだそれ自身の文化を持たず（ブルジョア小說の如きものを除き）、觀念と情操との表現に於て、否、屢〻觀念と情操そのものに於て、貴族階級を追想し、模倣しつゝあった。ロマンティシストたちは歷史のこの轉換期を感情的、感傷的に代表する人々であった。

それゆゑに彼等の後に出た中產市民階級の人々――ヴィクトリア朝のブルジョアたち――は一方に於てロマンティシストたちの業績（たとへそれが屢〻單なる夢に過ぎなかったとしても）に對して僞りなき愛惜の情を示しながらも、實際生活の危機に於ては彼等を信賴することができなかった。一八三〇年以後のイギリス人たちはフランス革命の失敗を見、一般に急激な社會改造

# 一　ヴィクトリアニズム

の運動に對して疑惑を持つやうになつた。（實を言へばロマンティシストたち自身、最初の期待と熱情との冷却とともに、フランス革命から背を向けた。）そしてその結果生まれたものがヴィクトリア朝の二重の冷淡或は無感覺――詩と革命、思想と實際運動とに對する反動――である。

「イギリス中産階級の人々は」とチェスタトンはその著「文學に於けるヴィクトリア朝」のなかで言ふ「詩を賞讚するのと殆んど同じほど詩を信用しなくなつた。彼等は一方に於ては詩的洞察力も、他方に於ては暴力も、どちらも實際的であるとは信じることができなかつた。彼等は『君たちは詩人は雲のなかにゐるといふが、雷電もやはり雲のなかにゐるのだ』といふヒューゴーの大なる警告に對して耳を貸さなかつた。理想は空虛のうちに消耗しつくされた。ヴィクトリア朝のイギリスは、愚かにも、もはや政治上の理想主義者と事をともにしようとはしなかつた。そしてその理由は、主として、これらの偉大なロマンティック詩人たちが若くてすばらしいにもかゝはらず、不妊症的な或るものを持つてゐたからである。汎神論者のシェリーは現實世界の波に

## 一 ヴィクトリアニズム

「さらはれ、バイロンはギリシァのために劍を拔いて死んだ」。(G.K. Chesterton, *The Victorian Age in Literature*, Home University Library, p.28.)

かくしてヴィクトリアンズは自ら自己を思想的に罰した。實際彼等はその思想缺乏により、彼等の充實した生活からさへフランスに於けるやうなリアリズムの文學を成長させることもできず、バルザックや、フローベールや、ゾラによつて自然主義の文學と文學理論が形成された時にも、それを正當に理解することができなかつた。

フランス革命よりも一世紀半前に、イギリスはピューリタン革命を持つた。この革命は成功した。しかしその成功は思想と文化に對する宗教的熱狂と武力の勝利の如き形式を執つた。フランス革命は、これに反して、失敗した。しかしフランスに於けるこの運動は、その失敗にもかゝはらず、根柢に思想を持ち、運動の途中と後とに思想を生んだ。イギリス人はこの革命に抵抗し、かく抵抗することに於て成功した。しかし同時に彼等は彼等の精神を枯渴せしめ、海外に於ける商業上の發展と反對に、文化的にはヨー

ロッパから孤立した。我々が前に引用した歴史家によれば、ヴィクトリア朝はマコーレイ(T. B. Macaulay, 1800-59)の登場から始まる。マコーレイはこの時代をかたちづくる二つのもの、「意識的な信條の安價で偏狹な點と、無意識な傳統の豐富で人間性に富める點」を代表する。言はゞ「そこには二人のマコーレイがあつた。一人は合理的なマコーレイで殆んど常に正しかつた。他の一人はロマンティックなマコーレイで殆んど常にまちがつてをり、從つてこの時代を取扱ふ作家たちが彼等の主人公をヴィクトリアンズらしく見せるためには、例へばゴールズワージーの「フォーサイト家物語」に出てくるソームズ(Soames)の如く、彼等を思想に於ては淺薄だが本能に於ては健全な人間として描きだすことを、性格描寫の一つのこつとしてゐるほどである。

そしてヴィクトリアンズの乏しい思想のうち唯一の明確な、首尾一貫せる

一　ヴィクトリアニズム

## 一 ヴィクトリアニズム

思想は、自由思想と個人主義、或は自由なる個人の觀念であつた。しかし自由とは如何なる自由であらうか。自由とは何ものかゞ何ものかに對して自由であることでなければならぬ。ロマンティシストによつて自由とは主觀的なものであり、人間の心情が現實の世界——貴族とブルジョアとの妥協が破れ、次第にブルジョア化してゆく社會——に對して自由なることであつた。しかし既にブルジョア社會が形成され、その社會に住んでゐたヴィクトリア朝の市民にとつて、彼等が自由であることを主張せんとする對象は彼等の社會ではなかつたであらう。それは國家であつたかも知れなかつた。たしかにヴィクトリアンズにとつて自由とは個人の企業に對する國家の不干涉を意味するところがあつた。しかし明らかに彼等は社會を否定しなかつたし、社會から離脫することをも欲しなかつた。そしてそれが彼等の信ずる唯一の幸福であつたが——社會に於てのほか實現する機會はなかつた。かくしてヴィクトリアンズにとつては最初から單なる個人主義は許されなかつた。彼等にとつて個人主義は孤立主義であるこ

— 10 —

とはできないで、一種の社會主義と並行することを強ひられ、個人と社會とを同時に存立せしめることが彼等に課された問題であつた。最大多數の最大幸福といふ妥協案、政治に於けるデモクラシーの思想はこの問題に對する一つの解答であつた。

しかし時の經過のうちにヴィクトリアンズの自由を制限するものが現れてきた。しかもこの自由と幸福との敵は、既に過去のものとなつた貴族でもなければ、次第に不吉な陰を投げ始めた無産階級でもなく、ヴィクトリアンズ自身の社會であることが明らかにされた。何故なら作られたものがかへつて作るものを司配するといふ歷史の公理がこゝにも妥當したからである。ヴィクトリア朝中産市民階級の經濟社會が必要として呼びだしたところの資本主義が次第に強化され、組織化されるに從ひ、それは一つの非人間的な機構と勢力を持ち、生みの親であるところの社會と社會のなかの個人を司配し、束縛しはじめた。國家の權力は個人の權利でなく、社會の繁榮は個人の幸福でないことが證明された。人々はもはや彼等自身の社會に於て自

一　ヴィクトリアニズム

## 一　ヴィクトリアニズム

由でなかった。そしてそれとともに彼等のすべての信條、すべての設立物が、その堅固な外觀にもかゝはらず、空虚になり、その空虚を認めまいとするところに虚偽が生れた。ヴィクトリアンズはもともと思想を蔑み、感情のデリカシーを笑ひ、文化を信用しなかった。彼等の強みは社會にあり、社會に於ける實際生活の充實にあった。しかるにその社會がゆきづまり、社會と個人との間に喰ひちがひができてから、ヴィクトリアンズはその誇りであった社會生活に於てさへ空疎になり、首尾一貫せざるものとなった。ヴィクトリアンズの墮落、彼等の意識的或は無意識な虚偽は、かくして、彼等の社會そのものの變質によって必然的に惹きおこされたものであった。

## 二　諷　刺

我々がこれまで辿つてきたやうなヴィクトリア朝イギリスに於ける二重性——內容と形式との相違、嚴めしい外觀の下に於ける實體の虛脫——は諷刺の好題目である。何故なら諷刺そのものが、言はゞ、二重の視力であり、すべての事物を表からと同時に裏から見る能力であるから。そしてサミュエル・バトラーがヴィクトリア朝に登場したのは折りよく諷刺家としてであつた。彼は人としての幸福はいづれともあれ、諷刺家として完成するに適當な境遇と經驗とを與へられた。年代的にほゞ正確にヴィクトリア女王の治世と終始した彼は、すべての道德のうへに宗教——たとへ名義上のものであらうとも——が君臨し、「家族の祈禱」ファミリー・プレイヤ——彼は後にそれをリアリスティックな、やゝユーモラスなタッチをもつて繪に描いた——が各戶に嚴めしく行はれてゐた頃、典型的な——よし必ずしも普通以上に惡くないにしても——牧師の

## 二　諷　刺

家に生まれ、ヴィクトリア朝イギリスの誇りであつたパブリック・スクールの一つ——バトラー自身の祖父によつて有名にされた豫備校——に送られ、ヴィクトリア朝の紳士とおそらくえせ紳士を養成した大學(ケンブリッヂ)で教育を受けた。彼はこれらすべてのものに就いて、そのからくりを知り、從つてそれらすべてのものから反撥した。諷刺家になるためには、その對象に對する正確な知識と強烈な關心を持つことが要求されるが、同時に彼と對象とのあひだに一定の間隔を保存することが必要である。諷刺家はその對象を充分よく觀察することができるために、對象に接近しなければならないけれども、同時に對照の一部ではなく全體を、表だけではなく裏をも見ることができるために、かへつて對象から退く。バトラーは半ば本能から、半ば外部の事情から、このやうな距離をその環境との間に保つた。彼は牧師の家にあつてこれになじまず、學生としては教室と運動場との雰圍氣から孤立した。彼は牧師として教育されながら、最後の際になつて聖職から遁れた。そしてまた地理的にも、彼は大學卒業後ニュー・ジーランドに移住し、

原始的な植民地の牧場にあつて、遙かに「文明」國の現狀をふりかへりみる機會を持つた。自發的な流謫の生活は五箇年間つゞいた。その後彼は倍加された興味と關心とをもつて故國に歸り、居をロンドンに定めたが、首府の中心(Clifford's Inn, Fleet Street)に住みながら、最後まで獨身者として牛ば隱遁の生活を送つた。そしてその間に彼が試みたすべてのもの——繪畫、音樂、科學、文學——に於て、彼は常にアマチュアとして殘り、その失敗も成功すらもすべてアマチュアリズムに起因した。

諷刺はかくしてバトラーの特殊な知惠となり、その要素は彼の中期を代表する「萬人の道」(The Way of All Flesh, publ.1903)や、晩年のより清澄な氣分を反映する「エリホン再訪」(Erewhon Revisited, 1901)のうちにも殘つてゐるが、その特性の最も純粹にあらはれてゐるのは初期の書きもの、「エリホン」(Erewhon, 1872)や「美しき港」(The Fair Haven, 1873)である。これらの著作に於けるバトラーの方法は、彼がとりあつかふ思想や觀念を、それぞれの傾向に從つて極端にまでおしすゝめ、かくすることによつてそれらの思想や觀念の本

二　諷　刺

## 二　諷　刺

質的な馬鹿馬鹿しさと不條理とを證明し、或は反對に、最初は馬鹿馬鹿しく滑稽にみえたものから思ひがけぬ眞理を探りだすといふ仕方である。この方法は一見無責任に、空想的にみえながら、實は最も批評的、客觀的な精神によつて貫かれてゐるのである。人は同じやうな方法と精神をカリカチュアリストや實驗科學者のうちに見いだす。カリカチュアリストは人の顏かたちを誇張して描き、科學者は自然の一部分をとつて顯微鏡下に擴大して見る。彼等がかくするのは對象の最も本質的な特徴をより明確な形式に於て把握せんがためである。そしてバトラーがこの方法をヴィクトリアニズムに適用したとき、空虚なるものは空虚をあらはにし、虚僞なるものは虚僞の假面を剝がれた。しかし同時に、かゝる操作の間に、それまで日常の事物の蔭にかくれてゐたより深い意味は新しい光を浴びて生きがへり、戲れの逆説にすぎなかつたものから盡きざる眞理の泉が湧き出た。「エリホン」はヴィクトリアニズムに對する若いバトラーの批評であるとともに、彼のその後に於ける多方面な活動の端緒でもあつた。

二 諷刺

エリホン(Erewhon)は nowhere を逆に綴つた(wh は離すことのできない音の單位としてそのまゝ殘した)バトラーの新造語である。從つてそれは言葉の成立から言へば Utopia (＜ou, not＋topos, place)と同じく「無何有郷」を意味する。しかし「ユートピア」が普通「理想國」であるのに對して、バトラーの「エリホン」は諷刺の國である。そこにはヴィクトリア朝のイギリスが含んでゐたもろもろの僞善と罪惡とのパロディーがあるとともに、ふざけた外觀の下にかくされた眞理——パラドクシカルな眞理——がある。バトラーの心から常に去らない宗敎と敎會は、この物語に於ては、音樂銀行(Musical Bank)として揶揄されてゐる。音樂銀行は表面エリホンの國立銀行でありながら、社會の單なる飾物にされ、その内部からは事務の代りに音樂が聞こえ、實際に流通する貨幣は他の新興の銀行に奪はれてゐる。これに對してエリホン人が實際に信奉するものは女神イッドグラン(Goddess Ydgrun)——「世間體」の代名詞とされる Mrs. Grundy の名をもぢつたもの——である。バトラーはこれによつてヴィクトリア朝の敎會宗敎が陷つた世俗的墮落を諷刺するのであるが、彼

## 二 諷 刺

の次の言葉のうちには、キリスト教會の如く長い傳統を持つた精神的設立物に對する畏懼の念と、かくの如き感情からなされる理性の判斷中止がある。

「實際この建物(音樂銀行、即ちキリスト教會)は人の想像力に愬へると言つても誤りではなかつた。否、それ以上であつた――それは嵐のやうに想像と判斷とを同時に動かした。それは石と大理石との敍事詩であつた。それが私に與へた影響は非常に力强く、見てゐるうちに私は魅了され、心を和らげられた。私は遠い過去の存在を一層明らかに意識した。人は誰でも常に遠い過去の存在を知つてゐる。しかしその知識は、過去の生活を證明するやうなものの前に立つとき、最も活々したものになる。人間生活の長さに比べると、我々自身の生涯が如何に短いものであるかといふことを私は感じた。私はこれまでになく私自身の小さゝを感銘され、かくもおちついた建物をつくることができるほど常識の發達した人々ならば、どんな事柄に對する結論に於ても間違ひはなからうと信ずるやうになつた。たしかに

この銀行の通貨は正しいものに相違ないといふのが、その時に於ける私の感じであつた。」(Erewhon, Chap. XV.)

そして女神イッドグランの崇拜も、バトラーによつて必ずしも嘲笑されてゐるのでなく、彼はその高級な信奉者のうちに、イギリスの貴族や洗煉された上流階級に相當するものを見いだしてゐるのである。

さらに家長本位のイギリス家族制度は、エリホンに於ける誕生證文(birth formula)として諷刺される。エリホンの神話によれば、生まれたるものの世界とは別に、生まれざるものの世界 (the world of the unborn) がある。そこで不定の生活を送つてゐる子供の靈が、さまざまな警告にもかゝはらず、この世に生まれでることを望み、われから進んでこの世の青年男女二人を選び、現實の世界に赤ん坊として生んでもらふのである。子供たちはこのやうにしてその誕生の事情に於て兩親の恩惠を蒙つてゐる。從つて彼等は誕生とともに親に絶對服從をちかふ證文を入れ、十四歳の頃になつて今一度この證文を確認する。これはイギリスに於ける洗禮と堅信禮とを諷したも

## 二　諷　刺

のであるが、生まれざるものの國に關するプラトン的空想は、バトラーが後に生物の進化を生物の生きんとする本能によつて説明せんとした時、母の胎内に於ける胎兒の生長も胎兒自身の意志と知識とに依るとの思想にまで發展した。

さらにヴィクトリア朝イギリスの非實際的な大學教育はエリホンに於けるブリッヂフォード (Bridgeford≪Cambridge＋Oxford) の不合理大學 (Colleges of Unreason) によつて諷刺される。こゝで教へられるものは矛盾と回避との技術で、言語としては假設語 (hypothetical language) が尊ばれ、教師たちは自己發表恐怖症にかゝつてゐる。しかし不合理の尊重といふことのうちには、バトラーのより深い思想がかくされてゐる。如何なる眞理も專ら論理的に追及されるならば結局馬鹿馬鹿しいものになる。人間にとつて眞に役だつものは非合理的な中庸である。例へば、動物は人間と共通な生態と性情とを持つてゐるがゆゑに、これを人間の食用に供することが禁ぜられるならば、植物もまた動物との類似によつて食用に供することから守られねばならない。

かくては人間の生きる道がなくなるであらう。そしてこれはエリホンに於て實際起ったこととして、「動物の權利」並びに「植物の權利」に關する章のなかで描かれてゐる。

しかし諷刺の二重性とかゝる二重性から生まれる創造的な力とが最も典型的にあらはれてゐるのは、機械に關する贊否の兩説に於てであらう。バトラーは旣にニュー・ジーランドにある時ダーウィンの「種の起原」を讀み、それから與へられた感興によって機械反對の説 "Darwin among the Machines" (1863) を書き、後イギリスに歸ってから機械擁護の説 "Lucubratis Ebria" (1865) を發表したが、「エリホン」に於てはこれら二つのものが形を變へて「機械の書」"The Book of the Machines" として現れてゐる。人間によって作られた機械は今やかへつて人間を支配しようとしてゐる、このまゝ進んでゆけばやがて機械の時代が來、曾て人間が他の司配者を亡してこの世界の王者になつたやうに、彼の司配權は未來に於て機械によって奪はれるであらう、といふのが機械排斥論の主旨である。これに對して機械擁護論者は、機械を人間の體

二　諷　刺

## 二　諷　刺

外に延長せる手足と考へ、機械の發達はそのまゝ人間の勝利であると說く。そしてエリホンに於ては機械反對論が採用されて、それまで發達してゐたもろもろの機械を破棄してしまふのであるが、バトラーに於ては機械手足論から、後に說くやうに彼の特殊な生物進化論の端緒が生れた。

「エリホン」の翌年出版された「美しき港」に於てバトラーのサタイヤとアイロニーは一層隱微である。彼は諷刺の二重性を極度に發揮するために、この書の著者として John. Pickard Owen なる架空の人物を想定し、自らはその蔭にかくれてゐる。こゝで批評の對象になつてゐるのはキリスト敎、より精密に言へば、キリストの復活といふ一つの奇蹟のうへに立つてゐる宗教である。そして假想の著者オウェンは正當派の神學を辯護するために、異端の說をかゝげてこれを論破せんとするのであるが、その場合彼の誠實な企てに於て失敗し、かへつて懷疑論の重みに壓倒されるといふのがバトラーの狙ひどころである。たゞバトラーの取扱ひは非常に微妙であり、從つて人は屢〻この書の目的を表面通り正當派の擁護として受取るかも知れない。

しかしこの書の主旨を物語にしたとも考へられる「エリホン再訪」を参照するとき、バトラーの意圖は明白になる。そこでは或る誤つて奇蹟と考へられたものの周圍に凝集する信仰が取扱はれてゐるのであるが、作者はかゝる神祕的な要素と理想的な要素とを區別し、眞の宗敎を前者からひきはなして後者に結びつけようとする。

「われわれの宗敎はわれわれの前に一つの理想をかゝげ、われはみな心からこれを受けいれる。われわれの宗敎はまたわれわれに奇蹟についても語るが、大部分のものはこれを信じない。最もよき敎導者は理想的なるものに力を入れ、奇蹟は表面に出さないでおく。もしも彼等があけすけに現代はこれらの奇蹟を不必要にしたと言ふことができるならば、彼等はさう言ふであらう。しかし彼等はさう言はない方がよいのであらう。それにもかゝはらず、彼等の意見がよくわかつてもらへるやうに工夫し、聽き手はそれで滿足する。」(Erewhon Revisited, Chap. XXIV.)

以上に於て我々はバトラーの諷刺がほゞ如何なるものであるかを見てき

二 諷 刺

— 23 —

た。それは何より批評的であり、批評としていちじるしく否定的である。そしてこのやうな否定的な批評もまた存在の理由を持ち、歴史の或る時期に於ては特に必要である。何故なら我々の生活の全價値がそのなかに含まれてゐるところの歴史的現在は、過去のうへに立つ。しかし現在が過去のうへに立つといふことは、それが一面に於て過去の延長であるとともに、他面に於て過去の否定であるといふ意味を持つ。實際、われわれの現在が單に過去の總和にすぎないならば、それは過去に對して特に現在と呼ばれる理由は無いであらう。現在が常に危機であると言はれるのも、それが過去の持續とは異つた意味を持ち、過去を否定することにより未來との關係に於て自己の特殊な立場を建設しなければならないからであり、歴史の轉換期とはこのやうな危機の大なるものに過ぎないのであらう。諷刺は歴史のかゝる時期に於て缺くことのできない否定の知惠としてはたらく。たゞその否定は正面からでなく、裏面からなされる。何故なら過去が否定される必要があるのは、それが時間的に切離されてゐるのでなく、因襲や制度

や觀念として現在のうちに存續してゐるからであり、かく現在のうちに含まれた過去を否定するのは容易でない。よしこれを正面から否定することが不可能でないまでも、屢〻かくすることによつてこれに不必要な重大性を與へる結果になる。さればバトラーが諷刺家としてヴィクトリアニズムに對したとき、彼は別の方法をとつた。彼は言はゞ對象を叱責してこれを沈默させるのでなく、かへつて對象を煽てて得意に喋らせ、かくすることのうちに曝露する對象の不條理と自家撞著とを心から笑つた。しかしその笑ひは最も批評的な笑ひであり、かく笑はれたとき對象は審判され、もはや再びひとりすがることのできないやうに突きはなされてゐるのである。

この點で諷刺とユーモアとは正反對な態度であるといふことができる。ユーモアは諷刺と同じく二重の洞察力であり、その方法として誇張と、屢〻その反對物である縮小と、顚倒或は裏返し(inside out)の手續を用ゐる。しかし諷刺が知的であるのに對して、ユーモアは情的であり、前者が否定と排棄の態度であるのに對して、後者は肯定と受容の態度である。ユーモリス

二 諷 刺

## 二　諷　刺

トが如何にしても對象を辯護することができない時には、彼はその否定のうちに自分自身をも含め、かくして否定の鋒先をやはらげ、いやしくも否定しなければならないといふことに對する言ひわけをする。諷刺家の言ひわけは——もしも彼がその辛辣な否定的態度について言ひわけをしなければならないとすれば——歷史のうちにある。ユーモアは和解と統一の時代のものであり、諷刺は對立と分離の時代のものである。如何に統一が望ましいにしても、それは分離すべきものが分離した後でなければ不可能であり、ユーモリストが敵をも愛し、時代との關係に於て懷古的であるとき、諷刺家はすべての情を殺して理性の冷い光に賴り、過去に背を向けて現實の批判に向ふ。

しかしバトラーの諷刺は單なる否定に終らなかつた。それは生命的であり、屢〻積極的な眞理を創造した。實際バトラーに於て諷刺の二重性は思惟の一種の辯證法であつた。彼はいたるところに矛盾と對立を見、それゆゑにかへつてそこに新しい綜合の可能を見いだした。如何なる眞理も極端に

おしすゝめられて不合理にならぬものはなく、平凡なもの、不合理と見えるものすら裏返しにすることによつて屢〻思ひがけぬ眞理になつた。かゝる二重の世界に於ては、否定は肯定に連なり、批評は新しい創造の端緒となつた。そしてバトラーに於てこのやうな創造の最も偉大なものは、ダーウィニズムのパロディー（よし無意識のものであり、或は善意のものであらうとも）から始まつてダーウィニズムの顚倒に終つた新ラマルク主義的進化論であるが、彼の文學的リアリズムもまた結局諷刺の精神から生まれたといふことができる。

## 二　諷刺

　何故なら諷刺は辯證法として思惟の一つの論理であるとともに、また想像力の形式として一つの藝術的方法でもあるからである。諷刺が二重の視力であり、事物を表からと同時に裏から見るといふことは、言ひかへればそれが事物を立體的に見るといふことである。しかるにものを立體的に見るといふことは、とりもなほさず、ものを藝術的或は文學的に見るといふことである。文學的描寫が他の記述と異るのは、後者が説明として必然的

## 二 諷 刺

に平板であるのに對して、前者が事物を三次元の世界に於てあるが如くに見、これを構成的に描きだす點にある。もつとも諷刺の世界は理知の世界であつて、情操の世界ではない。知力の光はすべてのものに透(す)きとほり、その光の司配するところ事物の立體性を直接に證明する明暗の對照はない。ロマンティシズムの文學に於ては問題が簡單である。この主觀的な文學は情操それ自身の陰影を客觀的事物の投影に代用する。しかし情操のほの暗い蔭のみが文學的なるものではない。文學はなんらかの形式に於ける情操の表白であり、知性の協力なしには文學は狹い主觀の制限を越えて廣い客觀的世界の像となることはできない。そして諷刺的世界の透明な知力の光と乾いた空氣を住みにくゝ感じる人々は、諷刺文學に對して不滿を述べるよりも前に、彼等が育つてきたロマンティシズムの偏つた影響と、知的文學を呼びだした時代の趨勢を嘆ずべきであらう。

藝術品として見られたバトラーの諷刺的作品について言へば、「エリホン」

## 二 諷刺

は單に年代的順序に於てのみならず、その諷刺の適切さに於て、諷刺から生まれる想像的世界の仕上げに於て、その調子の高雅と雰圍氣の明朗さに於て、彼の類書中容易に第一位を占める。そこにあつてはすべての價値が顚倒し、常識の考へて賤しとするものが高められ、常識の尊しとするものが貶しめられてゐる。しかしそれは決して暗鬱な世界ではない。スウィフトの諷刺をあんなにも辛辣で絶望的なものにしたのは、それが宿命的と考へられる人間性の醜惡と、黨派心の入りこみやすい政治問題に向けられてゐるからである。しかるに「エリホン」には人間の愚行は取扱はれてゐるが、人間性は直接の問題とされず、社會はあるけれども政治はない。バトラーの取上げてゐるやうな人間或は社會の陋習は、人間の理性とおそらく笑ひの能力に愬へることによつて最も有效に是正されるのであらう。されば彼の諷刺は屢〻ユーモアと呼ぶにふさはしいものに和らげられ、知力はその特性を失ふことなくして同情に近づき、物語の全體は批評と半ばうち興じた空想との縺れ戯れるうちに繰りひろげら

れ、名残り惜しく閉ぢられる。

名残り惜しく――この感情は讀者と同様に作者によってもわけもたれた。「エリホン」から二十九年後にバトラーは再び同じ話題をとりあげて「エリホン再訪」を書いた。後者の物語は前者の終つたところから始まり、前者の殘したもろもろの人物や事件は後者に於てひきつがれ、發展せしめられてゐる。かく「エリホン再訪」は物語の筋に於ては「エリホン」の續篇であるが、その氣分に於ては必ずしも先行者のあとを繼ぐものではない。三十七歳のバトラーと六十七歳のバトラーとでは、そこに人間の完成と、かゝる完成がともなふ犠牲からくる相違のあるのが當然である。生涯の門出に書かれた處女作「エリホン」には、その銳い現實的批評の精神にもかゝはらず、或る清新な驚異の氣持が溢れてゐる。死の前年に出版された「エリホン再訪」には驚異と、感興と、好奇心とのかはりに、成熟した知惠ともの思はしい反省とが司配してゐる。ジョン・ハリスの巧みな言ひまはしを借れば、「エリホン再訪」は「もとの新鮮さを失つた發見を恆久的なものとすべきの發見」であり、「エリホン」は「ひとつゞ

のにしようとする努力」である。(John E. Harris, Samuel Butler, p.89.)

そしてこれら両者に現れる人物の性格的相違も、物語の全體的雰圍氣の相違に劣らず著しい。兩者をつなぐ中心人物である探險家のヒッグス(Higgs)は、前の作に於てはヴィクトリア朝に普通な宗教的因襲を持つた人間であるが、後の作に於ては最も自由な合理的宗教觀の持主である。「エリホン」のなかに出てくる人物に共通に缺けてゐたものがあるとすれば、それは常識であつた。しかるに「エリホン再訪」のなかには廣教會派(Broad Churchism)を代表するダウニー博士(Dr. Downie)、以前は無性格な乙女にすぎなかつたイラム(Yram)、その夫である市長、イラムとヒッグスの間にできた子供のジョージ、ヒッグズ自身の如く常識と世間的な知惠の持主が現れ、彼等がジェスイット教を代表するハンキー教授(Prof. Hanky)や、儀式尊重主義(Ritualism)を代表するパンキー教授(Prof. Panky)を手玉にとり、狂信的な市民を背景として奇抜な、しかし惡意のない詭計や策略をめぐらす樣は、驚異の物語といふよりはむしろ王政復古期の風習喜劇(comedy of manners)に近いものがある。

二 諷刺

## 二 諷 刺

「美しき港」の藝術的價値はその序文として添へられた「故ジョン・ピッカード・オウェンの小傳」('Memoir of the late John Pickard Owen')にかゝつてゐる。バトラーはこの假想的人物の傳記に於て、後の小說を書く手習ひをした。サタイアと、ユーモアと、アイロニーとの調和、批評的精神と精確な觀察との結合、傳記的挿話の系列によつて思想を傳へ、思想によつて事實を導いてゆく手腕——これらのものは小規模ながら傑作「萬人の道」を思はせ、その準備となつたものである。しかし我々はこの小說に進む前に、バトラーの科學思想を吟味しなければならない。何故なら「萬人の道」はバトラーの進化論を具體化し、藝術化したものであるといふことができるからである。

# 三　科　學

バトラーは彼の科學研究を、彼らしく、科學に反對することから始めた。生涯を通じて反逆者であり、ヴィクトリア朝の社會的因襲を非難した彼は、ヴィクトリア朝の社會が發達させた科學に對しても攻擊者となつた。そしてその攻擊は人間主義の立場からなされた。科學がそのうへに立つ抽象的原理に從つて次第に人間から離れていつたとき、これを再び人間の立場にひきもどすのがバトラーの目的であつた。彼は誤れる抽象的な「科學的」科學に就いて言ふ。

「もしもそれが、言はゞ、我々がそのうへでスケートをしてゐる氷の表面を厚くするやうであるならば、文句はない。もしもそれが水の底に固い地面を見いだしさうと試み、或は見いだしたと公言するならば、それは全く間違つてゐる。我々の務めは、あたかも嚴寒が續いてゐるあひだは氷が厚く

なつてゆくやうに、我々の知識を上から下に擴張して、氷の表面を厚くしてゆくことにある。我々は底から上方に氷結するやうに試むべきではない」。

(*The Note-Books of Samuel Butler, p. 329.*)

・そしてバトラーが十九世紀の科學に對する反對をダーウィンの進化論に集中するやうになつた時にも、彼の思考の方法は彼のこのやうな科學觀と並行するものであつた。人は研究の端緒を過去に求め、時の流れに從つて過去から現在に來る。バトラーはこれに反して、研究の出發點を現在に置き現在から始めて過去に遡る。何故なら、より少く知つてゐるものによつてより多く知つてゐるものを説明するよりも、より多く知つてゐるものからより少く知つてゐるものを推測する方が、より自然でより確實な、從つてより科學的な方法ではないか。それゆゑにバトラーが機械と有機體との類似に氣づいた時、彼は彼が知つてゐる機械の發明と改善とによって有機體の成長を説明しようとした。機械と有機體、例へば人間の手足は、いづれも道具として共通な職能を持つ。機械が體外に延長された人間の手足であ

るとするならば、手足は體内の機械である。そして機械がそのあらゆる部分と構造とに於て人間の工夫によって作られたものであるやうに、手足もまた同じ工夫によって成長せしめられたものではなからうか。もちろん我々はいつ我々の手足を作つたといふ記憶を持たぬ。しかし我々の手足をつくり、現にそれを持つてゐるといふことが、手足の製作に關する我々の最も完全な知識を證明するものではないか。もしさうであるとするならば、無意識とは知識の缺乏ではなく、反對に知識の完全を示すのではないか。

そして無意識な能力――例へば我々が手足を作り肉體を成長させてゆく本能――は非常に長い習練の結果であり、遺傳とは無意識な記憶ではないか。

完全な知識と完全な無智は兩極に於て一致する。同じことが完全な意慾と意慾の完全な缺如、完全な記憶と完全な忘却とに就いても言はれる。何故なら我々が知識や、意志や、記憶について無意識なのは、我々がこれまで曾て知りもせねば欲しもしなかったためであるか、さもなければ、我々が非常によく知り強烈に意志する結果、もはやどちらも意識しなくなつた

三 科 學

ためである。

「意識的な知識と意慾は注意の状態であり、注意は未決定から生まれ、未決定は疑問をあらはし、疑問は不確實に連なり、不確實は無智を示す。それゆゑに意識的な知識或は意志はそれだけで多少とも新奇と疑問の存在を意味する」。(Life and Habit, The Complete Works, p. 18.)

我々が本能と呼ぶものは完全な知識のために無意識になつた能力である。そして本能の所有を我々は遺傳によつて説明する。即ち我々はこれこれの本能を祖先から遺傳され、またこれを我々の子孫に遺傳すると言ふ。しかし遺傳とはその傳達の忘却を意味するのでなく、むしろあまりに完全な記憶、その完全さのために無意識になつた記憶と考ふべきであらう。そしてこの思想は當然我々の同一性(identity)に關する他の一つの觀念を含み或は豫定する。即ち我々の生命や記憶は決して我々一代のものではなく、相次ぐあまたの世代にわたつてゐる。さもなければ本能と呼ばれる複雑にして精巧な能力が形成されることも不可能であれば、それが保存され、傳達さ

れることも不可能である。

　一般に我々は誕生をあまりに重く考へすぎる。なるほど誕生は個人の歷史に於けるいちじるしい出來事には相違ない。しかしそれは他のあまたの出來事、例へばそれ自身のうちに兩親から來る要素を結合する唯一の細胞として母の胎內に存在し始めることに比べるならば、また胎兒として手足や頭や眼や口を發達させてゆく成長の各〻の段階に比べるならば、決して驚くべき出來事とは言はれない。人は誕生をもつて生命の初めと言ふ。しかしもつとほんとうのことを言へば、それは我々が如何に生くべきかについて知らなくなる點である。何故なら胎兒の時代には我々は無意識に成長することができるけれども、ひとたび母の胎內から生れ出ると、我々は意識的な工夫なしには生きてゆけなくなるからである。しかし細胞が胎兒になつてゆく過程が無意識に、卽ち完全な知識をもつてなされるとすれば、その知識は細胞が相次ぐ祖先の各時代に祖先の生活としてなしてきた經驗の結果にほかならない。 *Life and Habit*, p. 60.)

三　科　學

かくして我々はわれわれの生命の初めとして、母の胎内に於ける一つの細胞ではなく原始細胞（primordial cell）を考へねばならなくなる。我々は原始細胞から生まれてきたばかりでなく、現に原始細胞である。その原始細胞は曾て死んだこともなければ、今後死ぬこともなく、わかれ出て世界のもろもろの生物となり、すべての生きものはそれと同一であり、お互ひにその一員である。(Ibid., p. 86.)

この觀念を追及するならば、生物學は宗教に連なるであらう。地球上のあらゆる生物は集まつて一つの「生命の木」を形づくる。しかるに各々の生物は細胞の集合體であり、細胞はそれぞれ生ける獨立體である。しからば我々がわれわれ自身と呼んでゐるものは、實はそれぞれ自己の獨立した生活をいとなむ微生物（細胞）の集合體にほかならず、それらの微生物は彼等が集つて形成してゐる我々といふ集合體の存在を知らない。それと同じことが我々と、われわれが集まつてかたちづくるところの生命の木との關係についても言はれないであらうか。我々はこの生命の木を一つの個性として認

めることもできなければ、その組織や範圍も知ることはできない。しかしそれにもかゝはらず、この生物の綜合體を一人の生ける神として想像することが不自然であらうか。この神の特徴は、それが肉體としてもろもろの生物を持つてゐることであり、その肉體の進化のうちに我々は神の受肉(Incarnation)の神祕を見ることができる。バトラーはこの神を「知られたる神」と呼ぶ。(God the Known and God the Unknown, p. 62.)

しかるにこの生物學的神がこの世に現れるためには、世界がそれに適するやうに造られねばならない。世界は生物を發生させ成長させるために水や空氣を供給されたのであらうか。もしもさうであるならば、そこには計劃があることになり、計劃のあるところ計劃者があり、我々の生物學的神の背後にはより大なる神があることになる。バトラーはこれを「知られざる神」と呼ぶ。

かくて宇宙には生命の四つの同心圓があるやうに考へられる。最も內部にあるものは我々の肉體をかたちづくる細胞である。これらの生物は我々

三 科 學

を知らず、我々も彼等を最近まで知らなかった。彼等は我々のうちに住み、われわれを一人の人間にかたちづくつてゐる。我々は彼等にとつて有機界と無機界から成る一つの世界であつて、彼等は自己を有機的世界に屬すると考へ、彼等とちがつたものを無機的と考へる。

我々は第二の圓をなし、同時に汎生物學的神の肉體をかたちづくる細胞である。第三の圓に就いては我々はそのたゞひとりの成員、卽ちこの地球の神を知つてゐるばかりである。しかし同時に我々は天空にあまたの星を見る。これらの星もまた我々の地球の如く生命にみち、神が住んでゐるとすれば、第四の圓はこれらの神々を構成因子とする知られざる神である。

この第四のものはたゞ類推によつてのみ考へられる巨大な神であるが、バトラーは後に有機界と無機界との區別を除去することによつて、さらにより廣大無邊な神を想像することができた。自然界に於て生と死とは互ひに入りまじつてゐる。そこには絕對的な生もなければ絕對的な死もなく、人は生のことを考へる時には死を考へざるを得ず、死を考へる時にはかへ

ってそれを生と呼んだ方がたやすい。

「確實な唯一のことは」とバトラーは誌す「有機界と無機界との區別が氣まゝなものだといふことである。ひとつびとつの分子を生きものと考へることから出發して、死を組合或は團體の解散であると結論する方が、死せる分子から出發してそのなかに生をもぐりこませることよりも、我々の他のもろもろの觀念と一致し、從つてもつと承認しやすい。それゆゑに、無機界と呼ばれるものは或る點まで生きてをり、或る範圍内で意識や、意慾や、聯合運動の力をそなへてゐると考へらるべきである。」(*Unconscious Memory*, p. 15.)

しからば人はいたるところに神を見るであらう。神が遍在するといふ言葉はあまりにも使ひふるされた表現である。しかしその同じ言葉が、バトラーの世界觀に於ては、その最も自然で合法的な意味を獲得する。神は生命のあるところに從ひ、生命は單に有機界のみならず無機界にまでひろがり、かかる有機界と無機界とのほかに宇宙がないとすれば、バトラーの考

三 科 學

へる神は究極に於て宇宙と同延になるのである。

本來の生物學に歸って言ふならば、生の本能を記憶と考へることによってバトラーは生物のさまざま現象を説明することができた。生は、例へば、記憶の連續であり、死はこれに反して記憶の中絶である。環境の或る程度の變化と經驗の多樣は生にとつて歡迎される。それは變化のうちにある類似によって記憶をよみがへらせ、また新しい記憶をつくることによって生を豐富にする。しかし環境があまりに急激に變化し、與へられた經驗があまりに新奇であつて、いかなる連想の手懸りも與へられず、その結果記憶が中斷されることになれば、我々は死ぬ。死が人を殺すのは新しい境遇の疎遠さによるのであり、我々が如何にしても過去の記憶と現在の經驗とを調和させることができない時、われわれは自己と自己の環境に對する認識と信頼とを失って死ぬのである。(Life and Habit, p. 153.)

バトラーはまた同じ原理によって祖先がへりの現象や、雜種(hybrid)の不妊性を説明する。隔世遺傳と稱せられる現象や、飼ひ馴らされた獸が幾代

かの後にもとの野獣の性質をあらはす現象は、記憶の復歸によって起る。これに反して記憶の混亂と中絶が見られるのは雜種の場合である。雜種には系統の異つた兩親の記憶が傳はり、それらの記憶の和解が困難なために、不妊であるか、不妊でないまでも生れた子の生活力が弱い。(*Life and Habit*, pp. 152-3, 168-9, 183, 192, etc.)

かく生物界に見られる諸現象に於て心的要素の優越を認めることの最も重大な結果は進化論の訂正である。バトラーは進化の理論に於て、言はゞ、自ら隔世遺傳を示現し、チャールズ・ダーヰン (Charles Darwin, 1809-82) からチャールズの祖父エラズマス・ダーヰン (Erasmus Darwin, 1731-1802) やラマルク (Jean Baptiste Lamarck, 1744-1829) の思想に歸っていった。バトラーに従へば、種の起原は既に或る知られざる原因から起つた變種の保存か絶滅かを決定する自然のはたらきのうちに求めらるべきではなく、變種を生じた原因のうちに求めらるべきであり、それらの原因はチャールズ・ダーヰンの所謂「自然淘汰」の背後に遡るべきである。「自然淘汰」なる概念はこれらの原因

が何であるかといふ説明ではなく、むしろそれに對する我々の無智をおほひかくすものにすぎない。しからば種の起原は變種の起原に求められるほかなく、變種の起原は外部の自然ではなく、生物自身のうちに――生物の變化する欲求とこれを滿足せしめんとする新しき工夫のうちに求められねばならない。勿論生物の欲求が變化するためには、環境の變化が豫定されねばならぬ。境遇の變化があつて初めて生物は欲求の變化を經驗し、その變化せる欲求を滿足せしめんがために新しい工夫をこらすのである。しかしその場合環境の變化は飽くまでも種の變異に對する機縁にすぎず、變異の力は生物自身の意慾と工夫、知惠とその保存としての記憶にある。そして種の變異とは生物の進化にほかならぬのであるから、進化の原動力はダーウィンの言ふやうに種の偶然な變化と自然の機械的選擇にあるのではなく、生物自身の有意的な知性のはたらきと無意識な記憶のうちによこたはつてゐるのである。(*Life and Habit*, pp.249-50, 258, 261, 263-6, 272, 274, etc.)

バトラーの進化論に於ける中心的な著作は「生と習慣」(*Life and Habit*) であ

る。この書物は一八七七年の暮に、その翌年の日附をもつて出版された。しかし生物學に對する彼の興味はその後も減退しなかつた。むしろそれはダーウィン及びその追隨者との間に於ける意見の相違とその結果ひきおこされた論爭によつて促進された。一八七九年には「新舊進化論」(*Evolution Old and New*)が出版された。バトラーはこの書に於て進化論の歷史をたどり、進化論を大別して機械的・無目的論的と生氣的・目的論的とし、後者をさらに分類して、一つは計劃者を宇宙並びに有機體の外に置き、他の一つはこれを生物並びに有機體の內部に認めるものであるとした。機械的進化論はチャールズ・ダーウィンのそれであり、目的論のうち外在的なるものはペイリーWilliam Paley, 1743-1805)その他の神學者によつて代表され、內在的なるものはビュッフォン(George Louis Leclerc Buffon, 1707-88)、エラズマス・ダーウィン、ラマルク等が提唱し、今バトラーが支持してゐるものである。一八八〇年に出版された「無意識の記憶」(*Unconscious Memory*)に於ては有機體と無機體との一致が主張され、記憶を振動(vibration)によつて說明せんとする試みがなされてゐる。

進化論に關するバトラーの最後の著作は「偶然か工夫か」(Luck, or Cunning? As the Main Means of Organic Modification)といふ名で一八八六年に出版された。この書に於てはダーウィン流の機械論と彼の主張する目的論との對立が尖銳化し、ために全體が論爭的な調子によつて貫かれてゐる。

バトラーの進化論はその時代に司配的であつた思想からあまりにかけはなれてゐたために、それが現れた當時にあつては進化論上の「變種」であるかの如く取扱はれた。しかし時代は變つた。今日彼の思想と特殊な思考の方法は單に生物學に於てのみならず哲學や心理學の諸方面に於て受けつがれ、機械的物質力に對する心的活動の優越を認める思想のうちには、よし直接バトラーの影響でなくとも、少くとも彼の模範が認められる。

「彼は」とバトラーに就いてすぐれた評傳を書いたスティルマン女史は言ふ「ショーにさきだつて生活力(life force)の理論を組みたて、ベルグソンにさきだつて創造的進化(creative evolution)の原理を組みたてた。彼はまた無意識に就いて考へ且つ書いたが、彼がこの觀念をとりあつかつた精神と語法に到つては

その後三・四十年間殆んど理解し得るものがなかつた。」(Clara G. Stillman, Samuel Butler, p. 128.)

生物學と進化論はバトラー自身にとつても生涯の大きな事件であつた。それに對する興味は處女作「エリホン」のうちに現れてゐるだけでなく、彼の宗教觀が彼の特殊な生物觀によつて著色されてゐることは既に述べたとほりである。同じやうに彼の社會觀や政治觀の如きも彼の進化論から影響を受けないではすまなかつた。何故なら人間社會の文明や機械の發明等は、バトラーに從へば、現在意識的段階を通過しつゝあり、從つて法律や政治や、機械などは發展の途上にある本能或は有機體と考へることができる。我々人間の本能や有機體も曾てはそのすべての活動に於て意識的であつた。たゞそれらのものは知識として自己を完成し、無意識になつた。我々の欲求との間に或る平衡を保つに及んで、無意識になつた。我々の知識や肉體はすべてかゝる無意識の平衡狀態に向つてあこがれるものであるが、同時にその狀態はもはや進步と改善との停止したことを示す。社會的慣習や機械もいつかはかゝ

三　科　學

る黄金時代に達するであらうが、幸か不幸かそれはなほ遠い將來のことである。(*Life and Habit*, pp. 198-200.) その時が來るまでは、政治や社會的幸福に關するすべての問題に於て人は妥協的態度を守ることが望ましい。あまりに大規模な實驗をしてもならないし、全然實驗をしないのもよくない。彼はあまり新しい觀念と古い觀念は、それらのものの間に連續せる同一性が感じられるやうに、漸進的で忍耐强い仕方によつてのみ融合される。このことは我々に中庸の德を敎へる。自然は或る一定の方向に進みたいと望む場合にも決して急がないし、またせきたてられることを厭ふ。彼女は彼女の願望に遲れる生物よりも、かへつてその先き廻りをする生物の方を一層嚴重に敗殘者或は違反者として選り除ける。自然は保守的自由主義者といふよりも、むしろ自由主義的保守主義者である。社會生活とその改善に關する諸問題に於てバトラーの忠言は、それゆゑに、思ひがけず、しかし彼の生物學的社會觀からは當然に、ポウプ(*An Essay on Criticism*)のそれと一致する。

Be not the first by whom the new are tried,

Nor yet the last to lay the old aside.

新を試みる最初の人となるなかれ、
舊を捨つる最後の人ともなるなかれ。

## 三 科 學

## 四 「萬人の道」

我々がこれまで辿つてきたやうな生物學的進化論的思想を藝術化したものが小説「萬人の道」(The Way of All Flesh)である。この作はバトラーの死んだ翌年、一九〇三年に出版された。しかしそれが實際に書かれたのは一八七二年から一八八四年の間であり、この時期はバトラーの生物學的興味の最も旺盛な時代であつた。されば「萬人の道」は本能と遺傳を主題にした一つの生物學的小説であるが、それが同じやうな題目をとりあつかつたゾラの「ルーゴン・マッカール叢書」や、イプセンの「幽靈」や、トマス・ハーディーの「本性復歸」(The Return of the Native)と異るのは、本能と遺傳がバトラーの小説に於ては否定的・破壞的な力としてとらへられることなく、反對に積極的・建設的な原理として考へられてゐる點である。十九世紀の他の自然主義作家たちは個性のうちに遺傳される肉體的・精神的特質を、個性よりも強い、そして屢々個

性を破滅させる或る運命的な影響と考へた。しかるにバトラーはそれらのものを個性確立の原理と考へ、個性が環境と戰つて自己を成長せしめてゆく生命の基本的な力と見なした。このことは彼の作品を單に一つの生物學的小說にとゞまることなく、個性の發展を描く性格小說にし、同時に個性が置かれた環境としての社會をとりあつかふ一種の社會小說にした。

さらに附加的な興味として「萬人の道」は著者の自傳的要素を含む。勿論われわれはこの言葉を内面的な意味に解すべきであつて、主人公の身のうへに起つた事件を悉く作者の經歷におしつけることはできないのであるけれども、作者の思想感情の多くのものが主人公アーネスト (Ernest) のうちに移入されてゐることは否定できない。のみならず作者の主觀を反映するものはアーネストだけでなく、アーネストの後見人で同時にこの小說の話し手であるオウヴァートン (Overton) もまた作者の分身である。これらの二人は相合して作者の生涯と思想を表象し、彼等の相互に於ける關係は、既にスティルマン女史の指摘してゐるやうに、アーネストがバトラーの生活を生活す

四 「萬人の道」

— 51 —

## 四 「萬人の道」

ることによつて彼を代表するとすれば、オウヴァートンはその生活をふりかへりみる老成したバトラーを代表する。(Clara G. Stillman, op. cit., p. 191.) バトラーはこの小説に於て個性と環境、本能的知惠と因襲的觀念との爭鬪を描くために、視野を四代にわたる家族の生活にひろげた。今その家系圖を示せば次のとほりである。

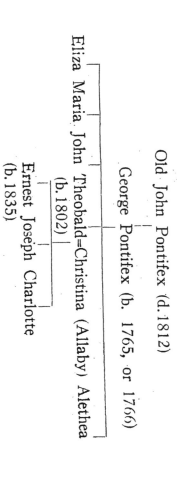

物語は主人公アーネスト(一八三五年生れ)の曾祖父から始まる。十八世紀の終り、イギリスの産業革命が始まつて、産業の中心が農業から商業に、手工業から機械工業に移らうとしてゐた頃、ロンドンから五十哩ばかり離

— 52 —

れた田舎に大工のポンティフェクス (Pontifex) 夫婦が住んでゐた。ポンティフェックス老は日傭人夫から次第に立身して九〇エイカーほどの土地を持つ棟梁になった男で、繪もかけば音樂もわかり、ユーモアも解する人物であった。彼の妻はがむしゃらだが信頼のおける誠實な女で、やはり人から好かれ、尊敬される性質を持ってゐた。

この夫婦のあひだに十五年ぶりに子供が生まれ、それが當時に於けるイギリス王の名をとってジョージ (George) と名づけられる。ジョージは小さい時から利にさとい、ぬけめのない男で、強い意志を持ち、後ロンドンに出て出版業者として成功する。彼は父のポンティフェックス老が本能的に深い無意識な確信をもってなしたことを、個人的な經驗によってためされた意識的な原理によって處理するやうな男であった。そして彼の成功の原因は、彼がその才能のほどを隣人たちから理解される程度に隣人たちを凌駕し、しかし決して隣人たちを當惑させるほどに隔絶した才能を持ってゐなかったことにある。

四 「萬人の道」

四 「萬人の道」

世間的に成功したジョージは家庭に於ては暴君であり、子供たちは親の愛を經驗することなく、冷酷な雰圍氣のうちに育てられる。なかでも最大の犧牲者はシオボールド (Theobald, b. 1802) である。彼は親と兄や姉の制壓の下にいぢけて成長し、牧師になる豫定でケンブリッヂに送られる。僧職に就く前になつてシオボールドは自己の使命に對して躊躇を感じるけれども、父親に威嚇されて牧師になり、また心からの愛情によつてゞはなく、むしろ他人の仕掛けた計劃にのせられて、牧師の娘クリスティーナ (Christina) と結婚する。

シオボールドはかく外部の影響に對して受動的で、自分が牧師になつたのも内からの要求に基づいたのではなかつたけれども、或はむしろそれ故に、ひとたびその職に就いてからは彼は全く十九世紀の典型的な牧師になつた。實際ポンティフェックス老が大工として手工業者であり、ジョージがブルジョアの典型であるとするならば、シオボールドはブルジョア社會のすべての偏見と制限を持ち、根強い物慾とこれをおほひかくす宗教的・道德的虛飾を

そなへた代表的な似而非紳士であつた。シオボールドは父から受けた冷酷な取扱ひを子供のアーネストに報いる。アーネストはそれがために父にも劣らぬみじめな少年時代をすごす。母のクリスティーナは人間としては惡くないが、夫を無上の人物と信じ、夫と子供との對立に於ては常にきまつて夫の側についた。

家庭に於て惠まれなかつたアーネストは、彼が送られた豫備校（パブリック・スクール）の生活に於ても不幸であつた。この時代の彼にとつて唯一の慰めは伯母のアリシア(Alethea)に可愛がられることであつた。しかしその伯母も間もなく死ぬ。伯母はアーネストが二十八歳になつた時に渡すやうにと、彼女の戀人でシオボールドの友人であるオウヴァートンに遺産を托する。

アーネストはその後ケンブリッヂに進み、卒業後聖職に就き、牧師補としてロンドンの貧民窟に赴任する。彼はこゝで同僚のプライヤー(Pryer)といふ男に瞞されて持金の殆んど全部を失つてしまふ。そして最初に始めた同宿人たちの教化にも失敗し、ふとした出來心から下宿の或るいかゞはしい

四　「萬人の道」

— 55 —

女に手を出し、騒ぎたてられて入獄する。獄中でアーネストは高熱におそはれ、危く命をとりとめるが、親からは殆んど勘當同然になる。しかしそれがためにこれまでの不愉快な親子關係から解放され、心機一轉し、ほんとうの自己を見いだしたやうな氣持になつて彼は出獄する。

アーネストの受難は、しかしながら、そこで終つたのではなかつた。不幸は次ぎに結婚生活の形をとつて現れる。アーネストは出獄後仕事を探してゐるうちに、曾て少年の頃ふとしたゆきがかりから恩義を與へたことのある以前の下婢エレン（Ellen）に出會ひ、オゥヴァートンの世話でこの女と結婚し、古着屋を始める。二人の間には子供まで生まれて、アーネストは暫らく幸福な日を送る。しかしエレンは飲酒癖のあるしたゝかな女で、遂に店の方もたちゆかなくなる。後になつてエレンが二重結婚をしてゐることがわかり、アーネストは危くこの結婚の絆から遁れることができた。彼はかくして、先きに親子關係から解放されたやうに、今また夫婦關係からも解放され、初めて自由な人間になる。その後彼が滿二十八歳に達したとき、

四 「萬人の道」

彼はそれまでオウヴァートンの保管してゐた伯母の遺産を受取る。かくして經濟上の心配がなくなつた彼は文筆の道に向ひ、俗受けのせぬ、しかし狭い知人の範圍では好愛される特色ある文士となつた。

以上述べたのが「萬人の道」の荒筋であるが、これに就いて我々は如何に考ふべきであらうか。この小説は一應環境に對する本能の反撥、社會的因襲に對する自我の爭鬪とその究極に於ける勝利を描いたものであると言ふことができる。環境は先づ家庭として現れ、アーネストはヴィクトリア朝の最も惡い兩親の見本を持たされる。これら兩親の影響は、彼等が子供の恣意を矯めるとと稱してその經濟的、精神的、個性的獨立を妨げ或は遲らせるところに感得される。しかし彼等は人間として特に惡い人々ではない。シオボールドの過失はたゞ彼が父から受けたものを子に移してゐることに過ぎず、クリスティーナのそれは彼女が夫を盲信し、夫のするすべてのことを無批判に是認してゐる點にある。しからば作者自身が言ふやうに、惡いのは支持ではなく、彼等にかくふるまはせる社會であり、社會の組織と因襲で

## 四 「萬人の道」

ある。環境はこゝに於て家庭から社會にひろがる。アーネストが眞に當面するものは單なる個人としての父や母ではなく、その背後にある宗教、道德、教育、經濟等社會的なるすべてのものであり、彼は内なる個性的な力のすべてをつくしてこれと戰ふことを要求される。「萬人の道」はそれとともに家庭小說から社會小說に移り、バトラーの批評的、諷刺的才能はそれにふさはしい活舞臺――虚僞と矛盾にみちたヴィクトリア朝の中產市民社會――を提供される。

しかし本能或は個性と個性をとりまく環境との關係は單純に内と外との關係ではないのであらう。アーネストのうちには兩親、祖父母等々の性質が傳はり、彼は社會的因襲のうちにその無意識な信奉者として生まれる。言はゞ彼自身が肉體的に兩親、祖父母等々の延長であり、精神的に社會的因襲の一部である。彼が自己の最も内密な本能と信じてゐるものも、それが本能らしい本能、即ち無意識にまで完成された知慧であるならば、それは實はかへつて遠い祖先から世代を重ねて遺傳された經驗に過ぎない。社

會の因襲的觀念にいたつては、肉體的本能よりも遙かにもつと隱微な仕方で人の心のなかに入りこむ。

「如何に我々はわれわれの思想について無智であらう。なるほど我々はわれわれの反射運動 (reflex actions) に就いて知つてゐる。しかし我々の反射思想 (reflex reflections) に就いては知らない。人はいかにも自己の意識を誇る。我々はわれわれが風や、波や、隕石や、何故とも知らず成長する草木と異ることを自慢し、われわれが好んで使ふ言葉を借れば「理性の導きもなく」餌物を追つてさまよふ動物と異ることを誇る。我々はわれわれがしてゐること、また我々がなぜそれをしてゐるかといふことを承知してゐる、さうではないか、と人は言ふ。しかし我々の生活と我々から生まれる者の生活を主として型どるものは我々のより無意識な思想とより無意識な行爲であるといふ意見がこのごろ主張されてゐるが、この意見には或る眞理が含まれてゐるやうにみえる。」(The Way of All Flesh, Chap. V.)

## 四 「萬人の道」

されば内なるものも外にある、外なるものも内にひそむ。個性と環境と

の爭鬪は單に内と外との對立ではなく、屢〻内と内との葛藤である。「萬人の道」はそれゆゑに、より深い意味に於ては、アーネスト自身の靈の内面的な爭鬪史であると考へられる。言はゞそこには二人のアーネストが居る。一人はより長い人間的經驗と知識を持ち、從つてより深く無意識の底に沈めるアーネストであり、他の一人はせいぜい一代か二代の經驗を誇ることのできる意識的なアーネストである。前者の命令は誤ちがないけれども無言であり、後者は時代の社會的因襲の支持を受け、そのもつともらしさに於て雄辯である。アーネストの精神史は後者の獨占的司配から始まり、前者の遲い眼ざめとその僅かに贏ち得た最後の勝利をもつて終る。

「お前はいたるところ虛僞でとりまかれてゐる」と無意識なアーネストの沈默せる最初の抗議は豫備校生徒としてのアーネストに向つて言ふ。「それらの虛僞は選ばれたる人々をも瞞すであらう、もしも彼等が異常に油斷なく氣を配つてゐるのでなければ。お前が意識してゐる自我、お前が思考し反省するところの自我は、これらの虛僞を信じ、それらの虛僞に則つて行動

するやうにお前に命ずるであらう。このお前の意識的な自我は、アーネストよ、氣取り屋から生まれ、氣取りによつて訓練された氣取り屋にすぎぬ。私はそれがお前の行爲を型どることを許さぬ――もつともそれは疑ひもなく今後長い年月の間お前の言葉を型どるであらうが。お前のお父さんはお前を打擲するために今こゝに居ない。これはお前の生活狀態に於ける變化であり、從つてお前の行爲も變らねばならない。お前の眞の自我であるところの私に從へ、さうすればものごとは相當うまくゆくであらう。しかしもしもお前がお父さんと呼ばれるところの、あのお前の外面的な、眼にみえる、古い殼に耳を傾けるならば、私は神を憎めるものとしてお前をきぎれにひき裂いてお前の子孫三・四代の後にまで及ぶであらう。何故ならアーネストよ、私はお前を作つた神だからである。」(Chap. xxxi.)

かくて個性と環境、本能と社會的因襲との對立は、それをつきつめてゆけば、個性とその外部にあるものとの爭ひから、個性の内部に於ける矛盾、意識的なるものと無意識的なるものとの對立に轉化する。しかし同時に社

四 「萬人の道」

— 61 —

## 四 「萬人の道」

會的因襲――因襲的なるすべてのもの――を單に意識的と言つてしまふこともできない。かへつて因襲の特性はそれが無意識なることにあり、因襲の恐ろしさはその意識されざる司配力のうちにある。一般に我々がその價値を當然のことゝして疑つてもみないもの、我々がその妥當か否かを反省してみようともせぬ思考の方法のうちにこそ因襲と因襲の詭計は潛むのである。されば我々が因襲の虛僞と誤謬から遁れるためには、無意識ではなくかへつて最も集中された意識と意識的な思想に依らねばならない。實際我々がわれわれの最も奧深い本能を活かすことができるのも、我々の眼ざめた叡智の力によるのである。そして本能自身知識に反するものではなかつたか。かくしてバトラーに於て意識（知惠）と無意識（本能）とは相互に貫通する。意識はこれを追及してゆけば無意識になり、無意識を掘りさげてゆけば意識に達する。そして彼が推奬するものは單なる無意識でもなければ意識的な知惠でもなく、かへつて意識と無意識、知惠と本能との交錯

し補足しあふ心の自由な活動である。「本能によつて矯正されざる理性は理性によつて矯正されざる本能と同様によくない」とはバトラーが既に「エリホン」(Chap. xxvii.)のなかで述べた言葉である。

かく絶えず理性によつて矯正され、それ自身知性のはたらきにほかならないところの本能によつて生きんとする態度は、一つの最も徹底した合理主義であるといふことができる。何故なら本能的生活とは、バトラーの場合にあつては、理性を無視する生活ではなく、かへつて最も完全な、誤ちなき知識のうへに立つ生活であり、彼が生命の中心に本能を置く時、彼は生命を非合理的なものと見るのではなく、反對に生命の諸現象を知識によつて說明し、肉體をも精神によつて內部から照らしだそうとしてゐるのである。このやうな知識主義、合理主義が最も明確に現れるのは宗教に對する態度に於てゞある。「萬人の道」の主人公は獄中で病氣が輕快におもむいた時、新約聖書を主な研究の對象にする。そしてこの研究は「信じようとも信じまいとも欲することなく、たゞ信ずべきか信ずべからざるかを見いだす

四 「萬人の道」

ことのみを念願とする人」の立場からなされるのであるが、研究が進むにつれてアーネストは次第に無信仰に近づく。遂にあらゆる疑問が不可能になつた時、彼はキリストが死んで蘇り、雲のなかを上天に運ばれたといふやうな物語が今日公平な心を持つた人々からとうてい受けいれらるべくもないといふことを明らかに認め、結局「純粋にして単純な合理主義」(rationalism pure and simple)に達する。(Chap. lxiv.)

この合理主義は、しかしながら、決して単なる功利主義ではなく、かへつて信仰の一面を持つ。世には単なる推理によつては解決のできない多くの問題がある。真理とはものゝわかつた成功者の大多数にとつて好ましきもの」であるとしても、この真理の規準はあやふやであり、屢々それが決定することのできない例外にぶつつかる。そのやうな時われわれは論理よりもむしろ本能に従ふ。しかるにその本能とは何か。「現に見えぬものゝ證據を信ずる一種の信仰」——それが本能である。さればアーネストは宗教を捨てて合理主義に進み、本能を媒介として再び宗教的態度に歸り、「彼がもと出

發した點、即ち正しき者は信仰によつて生くといふ點に殆んど歸着した」といふことができる。

そして實際これが正しき者、即ち合理的な人々が日常の重要な出來事に於いて爲してゐることである。彼等は些細な事柄に就いては彼等自身の熟慮によつて決定する。しかしより重大な事柄――病氣の治療や、金錢の投資や、難局からの脫出等については、彼等はその能力をたゞ人傳てにのみ聞いてゐる人々に任せる。彼等は知識ではなく信仰によつて生活してゐるのである。およそ輕信といふことから最も遠いユークリッドですらもそれ以上に出ない。彼の最初の前提は如何にしても證明のできないものである。しかし彼の基礎は信仰である。信仰と權威とは、それゆゑに、他の何人にとつてもさうであるやうに、彼にとつても缺くことのできないものになつてゐる。(Chap. lxv.)

たゞ問題は現代の我々が如何なる信仰、或は何に對する信仰によつて生きてゆくべきかといふことである。「いづれにしてもキリスト敎の超自然的

## 四 「萬人の道」

要素に對する信仰によつてゞはない」とアーネストは答へる。しかし「或るものに對する彼の信仰——何であるかわからない、しかし今こそはつきりわからないが、正しきを正しとし、誤れるを誤りとする或るものが存在するといふ信仰は日ごとに強くなつていつた。」(Chap. lxix.)

我々はこのやうな信仰が結局いかなる宗教に導くかを知らず、そもそもこのやうな信仰が本來「宗教的」と呼ばれる資格があるかどうかを知らない。おそらくこの小説が書かれた年代から考へるならば、アーネストが達し得る唯一の神の觀念は、我々が既に前に辿つた進化論的神、「知られたる神」と「知られざる神」とのそれであらう。いづれにしてもアーネストとアーネストの作者にとつて重要なものは、宗教の致義でもなければその抽象的な原理でもなく、宗教が日常の生活に對して持つ實際的效果である。

「徐ろに日がたつてゆくにつれて、彼(アーネスト)はキリスト教とキリスト教の否定が結局他の兩極端と同じやうに一致することを悟るにいたつた。それは單に名義に關する爭ひであつて、實質に關する爭ひではなかつた。

實際に於てローマ教會と、イギリス教會とは同じ理想の標準を持ち、紳士に於て一致する。最も完全な紳士こそ最も完全な聖徒だからである。また彼は人が信仰の告白をしようと無信仰の告白をしようと、それを極端にまで推進めることなく、寛大な融通性(inconsistency)をもって遵奉してゆけば、大して問題でないといふことを悟つた。危險なのはドグマを支持する非安協性であつて、ドグマそれ自身でもなければ、ドグマの缺如でもない」。(Chap.: lxix.)

かくしてひとたび自己の體系に融通性の要素を導き入れたアーネストは「首尾一貫して首尾不一貫でないのにはあまりに首尾一貫した性質であつた」。(he was far too consistent not to be inconsistent consistently.)そして間もなく彼は「愛矯ある無頓着主義」(amiable indifferentism)に陷つた。愛矯ある無頓着主義、或は彼が他の場所で使つてゐる言葉によれば「非合理的合理主義」(irrational rationalism)とは、世界の矛盾を認め、かゝる矛盾と矛盾の認識のうへに自己の生活を建設してゆくことである。內部と外部とは、例へば、一應分離し、

四 「萬人の道」

— 67 —

四 「萬人の道」

我々の全體系はこの分離のうへに立つてゐる。しかしよく考へてみるならば、純粹に内なるものもなければ純粹に外なるものもなく、すべては同時に内でもあれば外でもあり、主觀でもあれば客觀でもある。
「この困難から遁れる最もよき道は内部と外部、主觀と客觀との區別が便利である時にはその區別に贊成し、一致が便利であるときには一致に味方することである。これは非論理的である。しかし極端なるもののみが論理的であり、そして常に馬鹿馬鹿しい。中庸のみが實地に應用でき、そして常に非論理的である。至高の裁決者は信仰であつて、論理ではない。あらゆる道はローマに通ずるといふ。そして私が曾て見たあらゆる哲學は結局何かひどい不條理に導くか、さもなければこれらの頁に於て既に一再ならず主張してきた結論、即ち正しき者は信仰によりて生くといふ結論に導く。言ひかへれば、ものゝわかつた人々は良心を滿足させるためにあまり多くの質問をすることなく、最も便利に解釋された經驗法 (rule of thumb) によつて生活するといふのがその結論である。どのやうな事實でもこれを極端に

まで推理してゆくならば、やがて以上のやうな結論に遁れない限り、何かわかりきった馬鹿馬鹿しさに終るほかない。」(Chap. lxix.)

アーネストが、そして思想に關する限り彼と同一人であるところのバトラーが、この小説に於て達したところの結論は、かくして、實際主義、常識主義、中庸主義であるが、このやうな態度に我々は見覺えがないであらうか。この態度こそはバトラーが「エリホン」に於て諷刺的に說き、その後彼がもろもろの生物學的著作や、生涯手許から離さなかつたノート・ブックに幾たびも繰返して言及し、暗示してきた生活の原理ではないか。してみれば彼は、彼の主人公が思想的遍歷を了へて出發點である信仰に歸つたやうに、彼が他の方法によつて達した結論にこの小說に於ても到達し、本來融通性或は首尾不一貫を主旨とする彼の哲學に哲學として必要な首尾一貫を與へたといふことができる。

## 四 「萬人の道」

バトラーはかく「萬人の道」に於て彼の思想に忠實であり、言はゞその思想の妥當性を一人の空想的人物の生活行路に於て實際に證明したといふこと

## 四 「萬人の道」

ができる。しかしそのことはこの作品が一つの問題小説として首尾一貫したものであるといふこと、即ちそれが含んでゐるもろもろの重要な問題に對して完全な解決を與へたといふことを意味するのではない。ジョンソン博士に對するボズウェルと同じ關係をバトラーに對して持つたヘンリー・フェスティング・ジョウンズは、「萬人の道」を「ヨブ記」や「オディッセイ」と同じやうに「善き人がさまざまな試練を經て最後に勝利を得る」物語であると言つてゐる。(Henry Festing Jones, Samuel Butler, vol. II, p. 1.) しかし果してさうであらうか。アーネストは彼が敵として戰つたものに對して公平に勝利を得たと言ひ得られるであらうか。なるほど彼は自己の本能に眼ざめ、個性のより深い要求を活かすことによつて社會的因襲の司配からまぬかれることができた。しかし因襲とは單なる觀念ではなく實體である。それは制度として家庭や、教會や、學校や、社會のあらゆる機構のなかに入り込み、實に社會そのものである。もしもそれが單に觀念的なものであつて、思想と思考の或るマンネリズムに過ぎないならば、それは個人の自覺といふが如きものによつて

破られるかも知れない。アーネストが主として戰ひ、彼の個人的轉心によつてそれから超脫することができたのは、このやうな思想上の束縛であつた。しかし因襲的觀念は因襲的制度として具體化し、かくの如き制度が現實の社會に存續する限り、その犧牲者は一人のアーネストの精神的救濟の如何にかゝはらず、いつまでも種がつきないであらう。實際アーネストは社會に勝つたのではなく、社會から逸脫したのにすぎない。彼が社會的に獨立したと考へた時、彼は孤獨な、賣れない、非實際的な作家になつてゐた。もちろん彼は社會的名聲を顧はず、著作の賣行きを顧慮しなかつた。しかし彼がかく社會を無視して悠々自適の生活を送ることができたのは、彼が經濟的に惠まれてゐたからであり、その金は彼が自分の能力によつて得たのではなく、伯母の遺產として思ひがけず「轉がりこんで」きたのである。しからば彼の誇り得る「勝利」の唯一の形式であるところの「獨立」すらもが全く僥倖によつて得られたものであり、もしもかくの如き偶然がなかつたならば我々は彼がどうなつたかを豫測することができない。Deus ex machina は

四 「萬人の道」

## 四 「萬人の道」

常に問題の解決ではなく、それからの回避である。バトラーの小説が最後に僥倖といふ神の出現を要請したといふことは、とりもなほさず作者の側に於ける敗北を意味する。「萬人の道」はその表面的な完結にもかゝはらず、それが中心的なテーマとして持つてゐる社會的因襲の打破と主人公の救濟とに就いては最後まで或るでたらめな、未解決なものを含んでゐる。制度或は組織としての社會的因襲はたゞ社會的實踐によつてのみ改善されることができる。そしてちやうどそのやうな社會的實踐がバトラーの生物學主義に於ては適當な位置と立場を與へられてゐないし、また與へられることができないのである。生物學主義に於て把握される人間は個人であり、或は個人ですらもなく個體或は個物である。なるほどすべての生物、生物として見られた人間は集まつて群をつくるであらう。しかしこのやうな群は單に個物の集合であつて、内部に組織を持ち、個人から成立しつゝかへつて個人を規定し司配する社會ではなく、從つてその成員である人間も眞の社會人とは言はれない。「エリホン」から「萬人の道」にいたるバトラーの

諸作に於て、金錢はあるけれども經濟がなく、慣習はあるけれども政治がないのはこの理由にもとづくと考へられる。何よりも生物學的集團は適當に歷史と呼ばれるものを持つことができない。なるほど人間はそこに於て本能を持ち、本能は遺傳され、遺傳は時間を豫想する。しかしその時間は單に連續するところの自然的時間であつて、社會と社會人が持つところの不連續的な歷史的時間ではない。社會に於て實踐する人間の時間は、過去から世代を通じて流れてくるのではなく、現在に於て切斷され、或はかへつて未來から過去へ逆流する。我々が實踐の立場に立つとき、われわれはもちろん過去を脊負つてはたらくのであるが、同時にその過去を否定し、未來を現在に於て豫料し或は「先取する」(anticipate)ことによつてのみ、現在と現在の危機に於ける「われ」を確立し、創造することができるのである。

バトラーの生物學主義も、それが彼の思惟する如くダーウィン流の機械的決定論と異つて一種の目的論である以上、そこには未來の觀念が含まれてゐる。しかしその未來は過去の引きつゞきであり、言はゞ過去の投影に過

四 「萬人の道」

## 四 「萬人の道」

ぎない。そこには如何にしても過去を切斷する否定の契機がない。そして人が實踐する時、彼はもちろん個人として實踐するほかないのであるが、その實踐が社會に於て效果を持つためには、彼は社會の歴史的必然に從ひ、社會の現實的力に協力してはたらかねばならない。しかるにバトラーの「社會」はもともと歴史的・具體的な社會ではなく、單に個體の偶然な集團に過ぎないのであるから、そこには實踐の基礎或は內容となるべきものが缺如してゐる。彼の小說に於て主人公の「實踐」がせいぜい個人の觀念的啓蒙運動にとゞまり、個人の精神を規定する社會の經濟的・政治的機構にはたらきかける社會的實踐になることができず、彼の小說そのものがその中心に或るぼやけた、ふたしかなものを殘してゐるのはこのやうな理由に依る。

「萬人の道」はかくして社會的因襲を個人の精神的問題としては一應解決したが、社會の現實的問題としては未解決のまゝ殘つた。そしてちやうどそのことがこの小說の持つ藝術的リアリズムの特徵並びに限界を示す。バトラーの小說が我々の心を强くうち、近代英文學のうちに特殊な高い位置を

要求するのはリアリズム文學としてゞある。リアリスティックな精神は既にバトラーの初期の諷刺的作品にあらはれてゐた。すべての諷刺は對象に對する正確な認識を可能にする客觀的な精神なしには成立しない。しかし諷刺は批評であつて再現 (representation) ではない。その目的は對象をその特徴と價値とに於て批判することにあつて、かくの如き批判の資料を提供することにはない。言ひかへれば、諷刺に於て與へられるものは實在の描寫ではなく、實在の觀念である。もちろんこの觀念はロマンティシズムの作品に於けるごとく、主觀の願望や空想によつて對象から游離せしめられたものではない。しかしなほそれは對象そのものではなく、對象と並行し、對象に代用される或るものである。ここに諷刺のまぬがれがたい靜止性或は平板性の原因がある。諷刺が二重の視力として一種の立體的世界をかたちづくり、かくしてそれ自身藝術となることは既に述べた。しかしこの世界は事物から抽象された觀念の世界であるがゆゑに、それはもはやそれ自身の内面的な力——作者も勝手にこれを變更することができず、かへつてすべ

四 「萬人の道」

## 四 「萬人の道」

ての賢明な作者が作の迫眞力としてこれに從ふところの必然性――をもつて成長することもできなければ、すべての事物が持つ光と蔭のさまざまな屈折――われわれはそれをロマンティックな文學における情操それ自身の陰影から區別しなければならない――を持つこともできない。

しかるに萬人の道に於てバトラーの精神は、言はゞ、存在と結婚した。彼は彼自身が批評するだけでなく、讀者にも批評の機會を與へた。批評はこゝに於ては存在を新しい角度と深さに於て見させるだけでなく、かくして再現された存在がさらに新たな批評の發足點となり得た。實際バトラーがこの小説に於て如何に「見る力」に賴り、何よりも忠實な觀察者たらんことを期したかは――そしてそのことは本質的に批評家たることゝ矛盾するものではない――彼の次ぎの言葉によつても知られる。

「この小説は想像的な出來事よりはむしろ私が現に起りつゝあるのを見た事柄の記錄を含む。」(Note-Books, p. 377.)

實際、想像力はバトラーの強みではなかつた。彼は自らそのことを認め

彼に特有な卒直さとユーモアとをもつて一人の親しい友人に書き送つてゐる。

「奇妙にも想像力のないすべての人々のやうに、私は自分が風邪をひくと、ほかの人々もみな風邪をひいてゐるのではないかといふ氣になる。それでゐて自分が風邪をひくまでは、私は實際誰も風邪などひかうとは思はなかつた。」(H. F. Jones, op. cit., vol. II, p. 3.)

かくしてバトラーが觀察力と一種の觀察力にほかならない客觀的想像力——もしも我々がそれをロマンティックな主觀的想像力から區別することができるとすれば——に賴つて描きだしたもろもろの人物のうち成功せるものは主人公のアーネストや、彼の思想的補助物であるオウヴァートンや、完全な女性の觀念を代表する伯母のアリシアのやうに內面的、反省的に取扱はれる人物ではなく、アーネストと對立し、或は彼の外にあつて彼から見られる側の人々である。アーネスト自身は家庭的、社會的抑壓の犧牲として最も同情さるべき立場にありながら、その執拗な自己中心主義、俗人を

四 「萬人の道」

排斥する本質的な俗人根情のために我々を反撥する。もちろん小説の主人公は完全な人間である必要もなければ、讀者の好意をひく人物である必要もない。しかし彼が作者の目的と計畫に反して讀者の共感に觸れないならば、それは小説そのものゝ由々しい缺陷になる。彼は作者によつて讀者の同情をひくやうには豫定されてゐない。實際彼の性格はひと目で見てほされるやうな單純なものでもなければ、人好きのするものでもない。それにもかゝはらず彼が結局子供との爭ひに屈服した弱い人間として現れる時、少くとも親子の關係に於ける犧牲者はアーネストではなくかへつてシオボールドであるやうな印象を我々に與へる。クリスティーナはその缺陷にもかゝはらず、殆んど一人の天使である。彼女は彼女が觸れるすべてのものにさゝやかな、しかし紛れもない光と暖みをもたらす。

バトラーの小説家的技巧のたくみさが最もよく現れてゐるのは、しかしながら、これらの主要人物ではなく、彼等をとりまく端役に於てゞある。

アーネストの曾祖父ポンティフェックス老とその妻は、この小説のなかで、無條件にわれわれの好意と嘆稱とを呼びおこす人物である。祖父ジョージもまた傲岸不屈な性質と無意識なユーモアとをもつて永く我々の記憶に殘る。強者に對しては弱く、弱者に對しては強い豫備校校長のスキナー博士（Dr. Skinner）や、おしやべりで徹底的な現實主義者である下宿の主婦ジップ（Mrs. Jupp）に到つては、殆んどディッケンズ或はシェイクスピアの作中に現れる人物を思はせる。

しかしバトラーのリアリズムはこゝで終る。彼が個人のみ描いて環境を描かないといふのではない。「萬人の道」の中心的なテーマは、既に繰りかへして述べたやうに、單なる個人ではなく、個人と空間的並びに時間的環境との關係である。そしてこの關係に對する考察に於てバトラーは確に十九世紀のリアリズム、所謂自然主義の傾向に從ひ、しかもそれから一歩前進した。何故ならロマンティシズムが環境を輕蔑し、環境から解放された「自由な」個人の情操を歌ったのに對して、自然主義小説は人間の足を大地におろ

四 「萬人の道」

## 四 「萬人の道」

させ、環境に於ける個性の生活を描いた。たゞ自然主義小説に於ては環境が或る固定的、運命的なものゝ如く考へられ、從つて環境が人間を規定する方面のみが強調されて、人間が環境をつくる方面が看却された。バトラーも環境の強い司配力を認めたが、同時に彼は眞理の他の一面をも見のがすことなく、環境に對する人間の優越性、環境そのものゝ可變性を主張した。個性と環境との相關關係、かくの如き關係に於ける人間の受動と能動は、かくしてバトラーの小説に於て、それまでのリアリズム文學が企て及ばなかつた解釋と表現とを與へられてゐるのである。しかしバトラーの環境は歷史社會に現實化することができず、從つてそのなかの個性も社會人に具體化することができなかつた。このことは單に「テーマ小説」が含む思想上の問題にとゞまらず、藝術としての小説の技術に關係する。何故なら個性が單に人間であるだけでなく社會人であり、社會の歷史に屬するとすれば、小説家はその歷史の見地に立つことによつて彼の取扱ふ人物に對する新しい理解に達し、かくの如き理解は新しい描寫の方法を要求し、かくし

て再現された人間の生活は逆に社會の歷史を動かす原動力の一つともなるであらう。靜的・個人的リアリズムから區別された意味に於ける動的・社會的リアリズムとはかくの如きものを言ふのである。しかしこのやうなものをバトラーに期待するのはあまりに過大な要求であり、それこそかへつて歷史を無視するとの誹りを招くかも知れない。何故ならバトラーの後にショーが出、ショーが老いた今日、僅かに一部の若い作家のうちにその要望が朧ろげに具體化されんとしてゐるものを、年代的に十九世紀に屬するバトラーに望むのは無理である。むしろ彼がリアリストとして立ち、そのリアリズムに於て自然主義的決定論から一步ふみだしたといふことだけで、彼は充分我々によつて記憶され、感謝される理由を持つのである。

四 「萬人の道」

## 五 晩年の諸作

「萬人の道」の完成とともにバトラーの生涯に於ける最も困難な、しかしおそらく最も收穫の多い時期は一應終結する。それはちやうどこの小説が主人公アーネストの生活鬪爭の終了とともにいちおう完結し、それから後は一種の長いエピログであるのに似てゐる。アーネストが經濟的に心配のなくなつたのは、一八八六年に父の財產を相續することによつてである。またこの小説の完成とほゞ同じ頃、さしも激しかつた進化論上の論爭もひとまづ鎭靜した。その後一九〇二年に於ける安らかな死にいたるまでの期間はバトラーにとつて比較的平穩な時代であり、その間になされた著作は、言はゞ、既に完成した一人の個性が心のおもむくまゝに生活の野をさまよつて集めた落穗のごときものである。

しかしこれらの書きもののうちにもバトラーの特性は強く現れてゐる。

彼は歴史から離脱し、すべての傳統と傳統的方法を無視した。彼は彼自ら認めるやうに、常にアマチュアであり、'enfant terrible'であつた。このことは彼の弱みであるとともに強みであり、少くとも彼の特殊な知力はこのやうな條件に於て發揮されなかつた。彼は彼がかりそめにも眼をむけたすべてのもののうちに何かしら一般の通念とは異つたものを見いだした。從つて彼の著作は常に發見と抗議の或るものを持ち、その興味は主として人間的なもの――隱れてゐるのが見いだされ、或は著者その人から移入された人間性――にかかつてゐた。

かくて、例へば、一八八八年に出版された「奉納物」(Ex Voto)は、それよりも七年前に刊行された「アルプスと聖殿」(Alps and Sanctuaries)とともに一種の旅行記或は名所案内にすぎない。しかし後者は生活の休日を樂しむ人の明るいユーモアと機智に富んだ觀察を含み、前者はレオナルドとミケランジェロのやうに一般に認められた巨匠ではなく、それまで全く顧みる人もなく

五 晩年の諸作

世に埋もれてゐた二人の藝術家(Gaudenzio Ferrari と Giovanni Tabachetti)をあたかも古い知人のやうに親しく紹介することによつて、アカデミックな世界に間接の抗議を提出せるものである。一八九六年に出版された「サミュエル・バトラー博士の傳記並びに書翰」(The Life and Letters of Dr. Samuel Butler)もまた一種の抗議と考へられる。しかしこの場合、その抗議は世間に對するものではなく、かへつて彼自身に對するものである。バトラーは自己の家族に對して強い反感を持ち、彼が「萬人の道」を書いた時にも、彼はアーネストの祖父を人好きのする人物としては描かなかつた。しかるに彼がその後祖父の人柄や事蹟を彼の手紙や生前彼を知つてゐた人々について調べたところ、彼は圖らずも祖父が實際的手腕と或る豐かな人間性をそなへた人物であることを見いだし、みづから自己の誤つた先入見を訂正する必要を感じた。たゞ彼は、モーアが言つてゐるやうに、「憎惡者としては善かつたが、愛好者としては惡かつた。」(P. E. More, "Samuel Butler of Erewhon", A New England Group and Others, Shelburne Essays xi, p. 170.)それがために彼が尊敬と愛情とを

もって書いたこの傳記は、彼の雜多な書物のうち殆んど唯一の面白くないものになつた。

「オデッシーの女流作家」(The Authoress of the Odyssey, 1896) と「シェイクスピアのソネット再考」(Shakespeare's Sonnets Reconsidered, 1899) はアカデミックな偏見(と思はれるもの)に對する人間のための抗議である。シェイクスピアの小曲集に就いては、バトラーはそれを單なる詩的練習と考へる一部學究の理論に反對して、そこに破れた不幸な友情の表現を認め或は讀みこんだ。

"Why didst thou promise such a beauteous day
And make me travel forth without my cloak?" (Sonnets, xxxiv.)
いかなれば君は日のうらゝかなるを約束し、
われをしてマントもつけで外出（そと）せしめたる。」

こゝで "beauteous day" を友情に於ける忠實、"cloak" を裏切りに對する用心 (C. Knox Pooler のソネット註釋參照)と解し、全體を詩的な言葉の綾（あや）として受取るのは普通の解釋であらう。しかしバトラーにとつて "without my cloak"

五　晩年の諸作

は文字どほり詩人がマントを着なかつたことを示し、その〈假設的な〉事實からバトラーは驚くべき精細な人間經驗の物語をつくりあげる。我々はかくバトラーが自ら事實或は事實の斷片と考へたものに固執し、これを綴りあはせ、一つの全體に組みたてるところに彼の具體的或は具體化的想像力を見いだすとともに、その想像力そのものの特殊な偏りと範圍の狹さを認めないではゐられない。

「著者の個性は我々にとつてその作品よりも興味がある」(*Note-Books*, p. 107)とバトラーは言ふ。そして彼は「オディッシー」のうちに一人の全く新しい著者を發見した。この敍事詩の作者は、彼に從へば、時代といふ抽象的なものでもなければ、ホーマーといふ盲目の男性でもなく、一人の女性——「オディッシー」のなかに出てくる王女ナウシカー(Nausicaa)である。バトラーのこの考へのうちには彼の生命主義(ヴィタリズム)と個性主義が強く現れてゐる。彼は曾て生物進化の根柢に生物自身の意欲と工夫力を置いた。それと同じやうに彼は一つの藝術品を考へる時にも、その中心に生ける個性、生ける人間の知惠と想

像力を設定した。もちろんすべての藝術品は人間によつてつくられ、その人間は共同の製作に於てすら個々にはたらくのであらう。しかし敍事詩――「オディシー」の如き敍事詩がまさに敍事詩であつて抒情詩でないのは、それが個人によつて書かれようと個人の集合によつて書かれてゐるからであり、としてはたらく綜合的な時代の綜合的な觀念によつて貫かれてゐるからとほしてはたらく綜合的な時代の綜合的な觀念によつて貫かれてゐるからであり、文學批評家の重要な務めは敍事詩にあらはれたこのやうな綜合的な觀念をさぐり、進んではそれをとほして時代の相貌を明らかにすることにあるのであらう。しかしかくの如きはバトラーの非歷史的傾向と相容れぬものであり、彼はシェイクスピアのソネットに就いて試みたと同じトリックを、彼が「オディシー」の著者と考へた一人の女性に就いて用ゐた。いづれにしても彼がこの仕事或は發見に就いて感じた喜びと興味は非常に强く、遂には彼を驅つて「イリアッド」(一八九八年)と「オディシー」(一九〇〇年)の現代化――彼自身の言葉によれば"Tottenham Court Road English"(下町英語)による翻譯――にまで導いた。

五　晩年の諸作

## 五　晩年の諸作

さらにバトラーの讀者にとって「オディッシーの女流作家」が含んでゐる附加的興味はその女性描寫にある。バトラーは生涯娶らなかった。もちろん彼が全然婦人を知らなかったといふのではない。彼はかつて異國の乙女にはかない情熱を感じたこともあり、同國の或る婦人――「萬人の道」の獎勵者並びに忠告者となつた Miss. E. M. Anne Savage ――との交渉は彼を彼の恐れる結婚にまで導くかと思はれた。しかしそれもこれも既に過ぎさつた昔のことである。今、既に死期の近い老作家は彼が古文書のなかに見いだした一人の若い女性に對してあたかも父が娘に感じるやうな慈しみぶかい、靜かな愛情を感じてゐる。

「ナウシカーに對するバトラーの態度は、全體として、美しくうら若い乙女に對する節度ある老人のそれに似てゐる。何といふ向ふ見ずな、荒々しい、一徹な娘であらう、と老人たちは思ふ。そして彼等は眼で彼女のあとを追ひ、無理もないとほゝ笑み、年とつた頭をふる。その樣子は婦人に對して慇懃でもあれば、をかしくもある。彼等は彼女のかはいゝ腕を自分た

ちの腕に組みあはせ、あたかも偶然のやうに、彼等の手を彼女の肩に置かうとする」(Malcolm Muggeridge, The Earnest Atheist: A Study of Samuel Butler, pp.248-9.)

「オディッシーの女流作家」がかくバトラーの想像的な娘に對する愛情を含んでゐるとすれば、「エリホン再訪」(一九〇一年)は彼の想像的な息子に對する殆んど溺愛ともいふべきものを含んでゐる。この書に於けるヒッグズはもはや異郷の探險家ではなく、心の故里に息子を訪ねてきた善良な父親であり、實在せぬ息子を探し求めるバトラー自身である。曾て文學に於ても實際の生活に於ても感情的な弱みを見せなかつたバトラーは、こゝに突然自制を失ひ、ヒッグズとその子ジョージとの關係に於て盡くるなき感傷にひたつてゐる。「エリホン再訪」はバトラーが生前出版した最後の書物である。それは彼が最初にとりあげた話題を受けついでこれを完成し、彼はこの書に於て生涯の定められた遍路を一巡した。實際彼の死はその翌年(一九〇二年)に起つたのである。しかしバトラーの書きものは以上で盡されたのではない。彼は生前常にノート・ブックを用意し、そのなかに隨時の感想を書きこんだ。こ

五　晩年の諸作

— 89 —

## 五　晩年の諸作

れらのノート・ブックは彼の死後二回にわたって彼の友人の手で出版された。
The Note-Books (edited by H. F. Jones, 1912) 及び Further Extracts from the Note-Books (edited by A. T. Bartholomew, 1934) がこれである。バトラーの著作はいづれも非形式的で、著述の作法といふが如きものは一般に無視されてゐる。しかしノート・ブックは最初から彼自身のために書かれたものであり、從つてそこには彼の全人格が最も赤裸々に現れてゐる。例へば我々はこれらのノート・ブックのうちに文藝批評家としてのバトラーを見いだす。ビュッフォン (Georges Louis Leclerc de Buffon, 1707-88) とともに「文は人である」ことを信じたバトラーは、すべての文學的虛飾を信ぜず、かくの如きものを含んだ文學に對して眞向から反對した。

「ウォールター・ペイター氏の文體は、私にとつては、年とつた婦人がマダム・レイチェルのところへ行つて、磨きをかけてもらつた顏のやうである。その花やかさは脂粉のお蔭にすぎず、にほひは櫻の花を思はせる。マシュー・アーノルド氏のにほひは山櫨(さんざし)の病的な**淡いかほり**に似てゐる。」(Note-Books, p. 184.)

次の批評はふざけた、わがまゝな擬似論理を含んでゐて、自ら稱する如く「文學に於けるいたづらつこ」の面影が躍如としてゐる。「いろいろと話した末、我々は次の結論に於て一致した。──ブレイクはダンテを研究するために六十になつてイタリー語を學んだから駄目だ、ダンテはヴァージルがひどく好きだつたから駄目なことがわかる。ヴァージルはテニスンが追つかけまはしたから駄目だ、そしてテニスンにいたつては──然り、テニスンのことは言はぬが花である。」(Ibid., p. 183.)

さらにノート・ブックのうちには社會批評家としてのバトラーがある。彼は生れと育ちのよきこと、一言にして言へば 'gentleman' であることを人間のこの世に於ける最高の美德とした。このやうな理想は社會を離れては實現しない。そして社會は慣習から成り、あくまでも慣習的なものである。しかしバトラーの「呪はれた」慧眼はもろもろの社會的因襲のあまりに空虚且つ虚僞なることを見ぬき、從つて彼の社會批評は常に諷刺的であり、彼自身 'gentleman' とは緣遠い一種の獨善主義者になつた。そこにはまた宗教批評

五 晩年の諸作

## 五 晩年の諸作

家としてのバトラーがある。彼は教會が社會と同じやうに或る非合理的なものを必要とすることを知つてゐた。しかし生れつきあまりにも合理的な彼——朝起きて髪を梳るにも、左へ幾度、右へ幾度といふやうにきめなければ氣のおさまらない彼——は、教會が含んでゐる非合理的なもののために遂に教會並びに教會宗教と和解することができず、直觀と本能との生活のうちに或る宗教的代用物を見いだした。さらにそこには科學者としてのバトラーがある。彼は科學的實驗にはたづさはらなかつた。しかし科學の理論的方面に於ては彼はダーウィンの如き一代の碩學と太刀打ができるほど科學的思考の世界に深入りした。それでゐて彼が科學を研究するのは科學そのもののためではなく、あくまでも人間のためであつた。彼はその建前から一方では「個人化された科學」("personified science")、卽ちダーウィン化され或はハックスリー化された科學に反對するとともに、他方では所謂「純粹」科學に反對し、「科學に對する不信任を科學的根據の上へに置くこと」(*Further Extracts from the Note-Books*, p. 112) をもつて自己の主なる科學的著作、一般に彼の科

學的研究の目的とした。

ノート・ブックに現れたバトラーはかくして驚くべき多方面な才能である。そして彼はそれら各々の才能と資格に於て殆んど專門家の域に達しながら、如何なる專門のうちに局限されることをも欲せず、最後までよき意味に於けるアマチュアとして殘り、アマチュアのみが享受することのできる自由を確保した。されば彼のノート・ブックは單なる才能の羅列ではなく、それらの才能を司配する個性の表現であり、かくの如きものとしてそれは十九世紀の後半に於ける一つの最も注目すべきヒューマン・ドキュメントである。

バトラーの我々に對する興味は、このやうにして、彼の個性にかゝつてゐる。彼は單にノート・ブックに於てのみならず、彼の文學的、科學的その他の書きものに於て常に人間として語り、すべてのものをそれが人間に對して持つ意義に於て評價した。されば彼が今みづから評價される番にあたつても、それは彼の人間的價値に於てなされるべきであらう。彼の人間性は決して深みのあるものではない。彼の感情は凡俗であり、彼の思想はなま

ぬるい。何よりもそこには人間性を眞に具體化し、これに社會的な效果を與へる歴史的自覺が缺けてゐる。それにもかゝはらず彼が一個の人間として近代に於ける人間の歴史のうちに記憶さるべきであるとすれば、それは彼が内と外、心と肉體、感情と思想、本能的な知惠と反省的な知惠との間に微妙な釣合を保ち、不思議に統制のとれた重厚な個性をかたちづくつてゐるからである。彼以後、人はさまざまな方面に於て新しい、そしておそらくより深刻な經驗をしたであらう。これを文藝に限つてみても、ジョイス(James Joyce)の無意識に於ける、ロレンス(D. H. Lawrence)の肉體に於ける、オールダス・ハックスリー(Aldous Huxley)の理知に於ける、ヴァージニア・ウルフ(Virginia Woolf)の心理に於ける實驗の如き、いづれもバトラーのうちに或る萌芽を持ちながら、それをバトラーの豫想だにしなかつた方向と深さに追及したものであると考へられる。ただ彼が保つてゐたやうな人格の統制はもはや見られなくなつた。我々の時代が危機にのぞんでゐるといふのも、より深い内面的な意味に於ては、かく人間が統一的な人格を失つたことに

ほかならないのであらう。もちろん現代の我々が性格的に分裂したのは、そこに社會的な原因があり、從つて我々が我々の失はれた自己を取りもどすためには、單なる個人的自覺ではなく、社會的實踐に依らねばならないのであらう。しかしかくの如き社會的實踐も結局は生ける個々の人間をとほしてなされるほかない。されば時代の內面的危機と外面的危機が相通ずるやうに、人間の個性的完成と社會的實踐は別々にあるのではなく、密接な相互關係にある。バトラーがこれらのものゝ一つを强調して他のものを充分徹底させなかつたことは、もとより彼の重大な缺點であるけれども、彼が個人的に示した個性の統制と釣合は現代に於てもなほ暗示的であり、そこに我々に對する彼の意義――歷史を無視した彼の歷史的價値があるのであらう。

## 五　晚年の諸作

# 年譜

1835 十二月四日、サミュエル・バトラー生まる。所は Nottinghamshire の Bingham の近く、Langar の牧師館。父は Rev. Thomas Butler, 母は Fanny Worsley, 祖父は 1789 年から 1836 年まで Shrewsbury School の校長を務め、後に Lichfield の僧正になった Dr. Samuel Butler. (Dickens: *Sketches by Boz*, First series, Wordsworth: *Yarrow Revisited and Other Poems* 出づ。Queen Victoria の卽位はこれより二年後なり。)

1843. 家族イタリーへ旅行す。(Carlyle: *Past and Present*, Ruskin: *Modern Painters*, vol. 1 出づ。Henry James 生まる。Southey 死し、Wordsworth 桂冠詩人となる。)

1846. 正月、Coventry の近く Allesley の學校へ入學す。

1848. Allesley を去って Shrewsbury の學校へ入學す。初めて Handel の音樂を聞いて生涯その熱情的な愛好者となる。(Macaulay: *History of England*, vols. I-II, Mill: *Principles of Political Economy* 出づ。Pre-Raphaelite Brotherhood 形成さる。Emily Brontë 死す。)

1853-4. 冬、再び家族とともにイタリーへ行き、古い巨匠の繪畫に興味をおぼえる。(1853. Arnold: *Poems*, Gaskell: *Cranford*, Kingsley: *Hypatia*, Thackeray: *English Humorists of the 18th Century* 出づ。クリミヤ戰爭始まる。)

1854. 十月、Cambridge の St. John's College に入學す。(Thoreau: *Walden* 出づ。Oscar Wilde 生まれ、F. W. J. Schelling 死す。)

1858. ベトラーの最初の書きもの 'On English Composition and Other Matters', St. John's College 學內誌 *The Eagle* に掲載さる。學位を得、僧職に就くことを拒絶す。(George Eliot: *Scenes of Clerical Life*, Morris: *Defence of Guenevere and Other Poems* 出づ。)

1859. 九月、ニュー・ジーランドに渡航し、牧羊を始む。ダーウィンの「種の起原」を讀む。(Darwin: *Origin of Species*, FitzGerald: *Rubáiyát of Omar Khayyám*, Meredith: *Ordeal of Richard Feverel*, Tennyson: *Idylls of the King* 出づ。イタリー獨立戰爭始まる。Bergson 生まる。)

1862. 十二月、ベトラー、'Darwin on the Origin of Species: a Dialogue' を ニュージーランドなる Canterbury の新聞 *The Press* に寄稿す。(Spencer: *A System*

1863. of Synthetic Philosophy: First Principles 出づ。Hauptmann, Maeterlinck, Schnitzler 生まれ、Hebbel: Nibelungen, Hugo: Les Misérables, Flaubert: Salambô, Turgenev: Fathers and Sons 出づ。)

バトラーが家郷に書き送った手紙を集めた A First Year in Canterbury Settlement 出版さる。'Darwin among the Machines,' The Press に掲載さる。(Longfellow: Tales of a Wayside Inn 出づ。Thackeray 死す。Renan: Vie be Jésus 出づ。)

1864. 六月、友人 C. P. Pauli と共にイギリスに歸る。ロンドン E. C. なる Clifford's Inn 十五號館に居を定め、繪畫の研究を始む。(Browning: Dramatis Personae, Newman: Apologia pro Vita Sua 出づ。Landor, Hawthorne 死す。)

1865. 七月、'Lucubratio Ebria', The Press に掲載さる。The Evidence for the Resurrection of Jesus Christ as given by the Four Evangelists critically examined 私刊さる。(Swinburne: Atalanta in Calydon, Whittier: Poems 出づ。)

1867. Newman Street なる Heatherley の美術學校に通ふ。初めて Charles Gogin に遇ふ。(Mark Twain: The Celebrated Jumping Frog 出づ。Baudelaire 死す。Marx: Das Kapital 第一卷出づ。)

— 98 —

1870-1. 初めて Miss Eliza Mary Anne Savage に遇ふ。(1870. Emerson: *Society and Solitude*, Rossetti: *Poems*, Wallace: *Natural Selection* 出づ。Dickens 死す。普佛戰爭始まる。1871. Darwin: *Descent of Man* 出づ。Proust, Valéry 生まる。)

1872. *Erewhon, or Over the Range* 出づ。Zola: *Les Rougon Macquart* 出始む。) (Darwin: *Expression of the Emotions in Man and Animals*, Hardy: *Under the Greenwood Tree*, Holmes: *The Poet at the Breakfast-Table* 出づ。)

1873. 母死す。*The Fair Haven* 出づ。(Bridges: *Poems*, Pater: *Studies in the Renaissance* 出づ。)

1874. 繪畫 'Mr. Heatherley's Holiday', Royal Academy に陳列さる。

1876. 初めて Henry Festing Jones に遇ふ。

1878. *Life and Habit* 出づ。(Lord Dunsany, John Masefield, Upton Sinclair 生まる。)

1879. *Evolution, Old and New* 出づ。(Henry James: *Daisy Miller*, Ibsen: *A Doll's House* 出づ。)

1880. *Unconscious Memory* 出づ。(Flaubert 死す。)

1882. *Alps and Sanctuaries of Piedmont and the Canton Ticino* 出づ。(Stevenson: *Treasure Island* 出づ。James Joyce, Virginia Woolf, T. E. Hulme 生まれ、Darwin, Rossetti, Emerson,

— 99 —

1883. Longfellow 死す。Handel に倣って音樂の作曲を始む。(Lang, Leaf, and Myers の Iliad 散文譯出づ。Marx, Turgeniev, Wagner 死す。Nietzsche: Also Sprach Zarathustra〔1891 年完成〕, Maupassant: Une Vie 出づ。)

1884. Selections from Previous Works 出づ。The Way of All Flesh 實質的に完成す。(Gilbert Cannan 生まる。)

1885. Miss Savage 死す。Gavottes, Minuets, Fugues, and other short pieces for the piano 出づ。(H. F Jones との共同制作。)(D. H. Lawrence, Sinclair Lewis, Ezra Pound 生まる。Hugo 死す。)

1886. 父死す。Cambridge University に於ける Slade Professorship of Fine Art の候補として立ち, 失敗す。(Gissing: Demos 出づ。Wyndham Lewis, Siegfried Sassoon 生まる。)

1887. Luck, or Cunning as the Main Means of Organic Modification? 出づ。書記並びに侍僕として Alfred Emery Cathie を雇ふ。(Rupert Brooke, Edith Sitwell 生まる。Huysmans: A Rebours 出づ。)

— 100 —

1888. *Ex Voto: an account of the Sacro Monte or New Jerusalem at Varallo Fesia* 出づ。寫眞を始む。*Narcissus: a cantata* 出づ。(H. F. Jones との共同制作。) (George Moore: *Confessions of a Young Man* 出づ。T. S. Eliot 生まれ、Arnold 死す。)

1888-90. 'Quis Desiderio………?' その他の書きものを The Universal Review に寄稿す。(1889. Yeats: *The Wanderings of Oisin* 出づ。Browning, G. M. Hopkins 死す。1890. Newman 死す。)

1892. *Odyssey* の著者並びに地理探究のためシシリーへ最初の旅行をなす。(Kipling: *Barrack-Room Ballads* 出づ。Richard Aldington, David Garnett, Elmer Rice 生まれ、Tennyson, Whitman 死す。Renan 死す。Hauptmann: *Weber*, Maeterlinck: *Pelléas et Mélisande* 出づ。)

1895. *Iliad* の地理探求のためギリシャ並びに the Troad へ旅行す。(Conrad: *Almayer's Folly*, Wells: *Time Machine* 出づ。T. H. Huxley 死す。)

1896. *The Life and Letters of Dr. Samuel Butler* 出づ。(A. E. Housman: *A Shropshire Lad* 出づ。Edmund Blunden, Ernest Hemingway 生まれ、Morris 死す。雑誌 *Savoy* 発刊さる。Verlaine 死す。)

1897. *The Authoress of the Odyssey* 出づ。C. P. Pauli 死す。(Tolstoy: *What is Art?* 出づ。)

1898. *The Iliad rendered into English Prose* 出づ。(Shaw: *Plays Pleasant and Unpleasant* 出づ。Beardsley 死す。Mallarmé 死す。)

1899. *Shakespeare's Sonnets reconsidered and in part rearranged* 出づ。(Symons: *The Symbolist Movement in Literature* 出づ。Noel Coward 生まる。Dublin に Irish Literary Theatre 創立さる。)

1900. *The Odyssey rendered into English prose* 出づ。(Ruskin, Wilde 死す。Nietzsche 死す。Freud: *Die Traumdeutung* 出づ。)

1901. *Erewhon* 新校訂版出づ。*Erewhon Revisited* 出づ。(Queen Victoria 死し、Edward VII 即位す。)

1902. 六月十八日、バトラー死す。(Masefield: *Salt Water Ballads* 出づ。Zola 死す。Gide: *L'Immoraliste* 出づ。)

1903. *The Way of All Flesh* 出づ。

1904. *Ulysses; an oratorio* 出づ。(H. F. Jones との共同制作。) *Essays on Life, Art, and Science* 出づ。

1908. 第一回ニリホン晩餐會開かる。〔A. C. Fifield、バトラーの著作出版を

引受く。

1912. *The Note-Books of Samuel Butler* (H. F. Jones 編纂)出づ。

1913. *The Humour of Homer, and other Essays* 出づ。(これは1904年に出版された *Essays* に 'The Humour of Homer', 並びに G. F. Jones の筆になるバトラーの小傳を附加せるものなり。)

1914. 第六回目にして同時に最後のエリホン晩餐會開かる。*A First Year in Canterbury Settlement, with other Early Essays* (edited by R. A. Streatfield) 出づ。

1917. Cambridge の St. John's College 内に Butler Collection 創設さる。

1919. バトラーの遺著管理人 R. A. Streatfield 死し、その遺言によりバトラーの版權 H. F. Jones の手に移る。Jones の *Samuel Butler*; a memoir 出づ。

1921. 書肆 Jonathan Cape、バトラーの著作出版をひきうく。H. F. Jones と A. T. Bartholomew との共著 *The Samuel Butler Collection at St. John's College, Cambridge; a catalogue and a commentary* 出づ。

1923-6. H. F. Jones と A. T. Bartholomew との共同編纂になるバトラー全集

1925. R. J. Hoppé の *A Bibliography of the writings of Samuel Butler, and of writings about him* 出づ。

1928. H. F. Jones 死し, その遺言によりバトラーの版權 A. T. Bartholomew の手に移る。

1931. 十月, 雜誌 *Life and Letters* (edited by Desmond MacCarthy) バトラー特輯號を出し, 'Charles Paine Pauli and Samuel Butler', 'Unpublished Extracts from the Note-Books of Samuel Butler' を發表す。

1932. *Butleriana* (Nonesuch Press) 出づ。

1933. A. T. Bartholomew 死し, その遺言によりバトラーの版權 Geoffrey Keynes と Brian Hill の手に移る。

1934. *Further Extracts from the Note-Books of Samuel Butler* (A. T. Bartholomew 纂)出づ。

# 書誌

Hoppé, A. J.: *A Bibliography of the Writings of Samuel Butler and of Writings about him.* New York: Bowker. 1925. $6.

これはバトラーに関する書誌で最も詳しいものであるが、より簡単なものは後に挙げる H. F. Jones: *Samuel Butler: A Memoir* (Vol. 1, pp. xxi-xxx), Clara G. Stillman: *Samuel Butler: A Mid-Victorian Modern* (pp. 307-19) 等に見いだされる。殊に Stillman 女史のは 1932 年にいたるまでの新しい項目を含んでで便利である。

# 本　文

全集。

The Complete Works of Samuel Butler. Jonathan Cape. 18 vols. 7s. 6d. each. 但し
God the Known and God the Unknown だけは 5s. 内容は次の通りである。

Alps and Sanctuaries of Piedmont and the Canton Ticino.

Authoress of the Odyssey, The.

Erewhon; or Over the Range.

Erewhon Revisited; Twenty Years Later.

Evolution Old and New.

Ex-Voto: an Account of the Sacro Monte at Varallo-Sesia.

Fair Haven, The.

First Year in a Canterbury Settlement, A.

God the Known and God the Unknown.

Humour of Homer, The, and Other Essays on Life, Art and Science. With Biographical Sketch by H. Festing Jones.

Iliad of Homer, The. A Prose Translation.

*Life and Habit.*

*Luck or Cunning?*

*Note-Books of Samuel Butler, The.* With a Biographical Statement by H. Festing Jones.

*Odyssey, The.* A Prose Translation.

*Shakespeare's Sonnets Reconsidered.*

*Unconscious Memory.* With Introduction by Professor Hartog.

*Way of All Flesh, The.*

*Further Extracts from the Note-Books of Samuel Butler.* Chosen and edited by A. T. Bartholomew. 1934. Cape.

以上の外に今では次の書物が同じ裝釘、同じ賣價(7 s. 6 d.)で加はり、從つて全集は事實上十九册になつた。

全集に收められてゐないべトラーの著作には次のものがある。

*The Life and Letters of Dr. Samuel Butler.* 2 vols. 1896. John Murray. Out of print.

1931年十月に發行された雑誌 *Life and Letters* もまた多少の新資料を含ん

である。今その内容を示せば次の通りである。

Samuel Butler, by the Editor (Desmond MacCarthy). Pp. 235–51.

Charles Paine Pauli and Samuel Butler. Pp. 252–99.

これはベトラーが彼と彼の友人Pauliとの關係を敍したものである。二人の不思議な關係はベトラーの説明によつてもなほ容易に解きがたいものを含んでゐるが、ベトラーがシェイクスピアのソネットを考證した時、彼はシェイクスピアと'Mr. W. H.'との關係のうちに彼自身の經驗の或るものを讀みこみ、或は移入したと考へられる。

Unpublished Extracts from the Note-Books of Samuel Butler. Pp. 300–10.

Butleriana. Edited by A. T. Bartholomew. Nonesuch Press. 1932. 15s. (Pp. xvi+172.)

ベトラーのnote-booksからのselectionsで、雜誌 Life and Letters に掲載された

'C. P. Pauli and Samuel Butler' をも含む。

手紙。

Letters between Samuel Butler and Miss E. M. A. Savage. 1935. Cape. 10s. 6d.

Miss Savage はバトラーが Heatherley の畫塾で知りあった友人である。彼女は *The Way of All Flesh* の Miss Savage の親切な忠告者となり, この小説のなかに出てくる Earnest の伯母 Alethea は Miss Savage を理想化したものである。

バトラーの全集は分賣されてあるから, 讀者はそのうちから選擇して購入することができる。しかし彼の主な作品は全集版に依らなくても, 次のような安い叢書類で求められる。

*Erewhon.* (Travellers' Library, Penguin Books. *Erewhon Revisited* とともに Every-man's Library に。)

*Erewhon Revisited.* (Travers' Library. *Erewhon* とともに Everyman's Library に。)

*The Way of All Flesh.* (Travellers' Library, Everyman's Library, Warld's Classics.)

*Selected Essays.* (Travellers' Library.)

*Selections from the Notebooks.* (〃)

日本で印刷されたものには *Erewhon*, edited with Introduction and Notes by K. Ishida (Kenkyusha, 1924) がある。また翻譯には「エレホン」(山本政喜氏譯) があっ

で, 岩波文庫に收められてある。

研　究　書

I. 單行本

1. Jones, Henry Festing : *Samuel Butler, Author of Erewhon. A Memoir.* 2 vols. Macmillan. 1919. 42s. Boswell の *Life of Johnson* を思はせるやうな詳しい傳記である。權威書には相違ないけれども, 上下千頁に近い分量が殆んどを全くバトラーの私生活の敍述にあてられてあるから, 上はど暇のある人でなければ推獎できない。Jones にはこの外バトラーに關する著作が數種あり, そのうち (2) は簡潔な傳記として便利である。

2. Jones, H. F. : *Samuel Butler. A Biographical Sketch.* Cape. 1921. 2s. 6d. 今この略傳は *Selected Essays*, by Samuel Butler (Travellers' Library) の序文として用ゐられてある。

3. Jones, H. F. : *Charles Darwin and Samuel Butler. A Step towards Reconciliation.*

4. Jones, H. F. and Bartholomew, A. T.: *The Samuel Butler Collection at St. John's College, Cambridge. A Catalogue and a Commentary.* Heffer. 1921. 7s. 6d. Pp. 58.

5. Cannan, Gilbert: *Samuel Butler. A Critical Study.* Secker. 1915. (7s.6d.) Out of print. 特殊な見地と特殊な文體を持つた批評書。著者は特にsatirist としてのバトラーに力を入れてある。Cannan の試論 "Satire" (*The Art and Craft of Letters.* Secker) もバトラーに關する言及を含み、多少の參考になるであらう。

6. Harris, John F.: *Samuel Butler. Author of Erewhon: The Man and his Work.* Grant Richards. 1916. (6s.) Out of print. Introducton に於てバトラーの背景をなせる Victorianism を敍述せる部分が參考になる。一般に brilliant ではないが穩健である。

7. Joad, C. E. M.: *Samuel Butler (1835-1902).* Parsons. The Road-maker Series. 1924. 4s. 6d. "Mr. Joad has produced not only an extremely readable monograph, but

one which attains to originality through its suggestiveness and point of view." (H. V. Routh, in *The Year's Work in English Studies*, Vol. vi, 1925.)

8. Lange, P. J. De : *Samuel Butler : Critic and Philosopher*. Zutphen (Netherlands) : Thieme. 1925. バトラーの思想を整理し、分類して示した書物。

9. Garnett, Mrs. R. S.: *Samuel Butler and his Family Relations*. Dent. 1926. (10s. 6d.) Out of print. バトラーが *The Way of All Flesh* その他で彼の家族のことを惡く書いたのに對して、家族の立場を辯護した書物。しかし Mrs. Garnett が引用した例證のうちに、かへつてバトラーの言動を justify するやうに思はれるものもある。

10. Farrington, B.: *Samuel Butler and the Odyssey*. Cape. 1929. 3s. 6d. バトラーが *The Authoress of the Odyssey* に於て提出した意見を是認し、擁護したパンフレット。

11. Meissner, von Paul : *Samuel Butler der jüngere : Eine Studie zur Kultur des ausgehenden Victorianismus*. Leipzig : Tauchnitz. 1931. RM. 14. "He (Meissner) makes

— 112 —

it quite clear that Victorianism was not a tendency but a conflict. The point of his essay is to shaw that Butler's activity falls into the transitional period at which two epochs touch. His ideas arise out of the nineteenth century and he prepares the way for the twentieth. To maintain this thesis, Meissner enters upon a surprisingly lucid and well-documented examination of his author's ideas, theories, and attitude." (H. V. Routh, in *The Year's Work in English Studies*, Vol. xii, 1931.)

12. Stillman, Clara G.: *Samuel Butler. A Mid-Victorian Modern*. Secker. 1932. 16 s. (8s. 6d. で特賣中。) バトラーの思想を現代と結びつけて評價した好書。批評的研究としておそらく最もすぐれたものである 卷末の bibliography も新しくて便利である。

13. 月川秋骨著『バトラー』。英米文學語傳叢書。研究社。豫約出版。

14. Rattray, R. F.: *Samuel Butler : A Chronicle and an Introduction*. Duckworth.1935. 5 s. 初學者のための手引きにすぎない。

15. Muggeridge, Malcolm : *The Earnest Atheist. A Study of Samuel Butler*. Eyre &

Spottiswoode. 10s. 6d. バトラーの個性と個人的な生活とほしての彼の思想や文學を見ようとしたもの。この書物は他には見られない多少の創見或は異見を含んでゐる。例へば，H. F. Jones はこれまでバトラーの忠實な友人で且つ忠實な傳記作者と考へられてきたが，Muggeridge は二人の關係に疑ひを挿しはさみ，彼等の友情がバトラーの晩年にいたつて罅を生じたと述べてゐる。

II. 單行本以外のもの
1. Shaw, George Bernard :

    Man and Superman. 1901–3.
    Major Barbara (Preface). 1905.
    Androcles and the Lion (Preface). 1916.
    Back to Methuselah (Preface). 1921.

    Shaw はバトラーの價値を最初に認めた文人の一人であり，彼自らバトラー的な多くのものを持つてゐる。彼は機會あるごとにバトラーのこ

— 114 —

とを同國人たちに吹聽してあるが、Major Barbara の序文はそれが書かれた年代(1905年)から考へて特に注目さるべきものである。「彼サミュエル・バトラーは」と彼はそのなかで言ふ「彼自身の活動した方面に於ては、十九世紀後半の最大なるイギリスの文人である。彼は宗敎に於ける良心的な無頓着主義 (Laodiceanism) と金錢の重要さに關する不斷の熱誠な意識の必要並びに道德的な所以を極むることなく敎へた。バトラーの死後に出版された『萬人の道德』の如くイギリスの生活に關する異常な研究が世間に於んどなんらの印象も與へず、またそれから數年後、バトラーの異常に淸新な、何ものにもとらはれることのない未來を見とほすブセンヤーチェニーの影響に就いて譯のわからぬことをしやべり、世間の人々はイッド・ドゥ・ミュッセやジョルジュ・サンドを引合ひに出さなかったのがまだしもだつたことなどと考へると、私は災火に照つくべく絕望したくなる。」

2. Sinclair, May: *A Defence of Idealism : Some Questions and Conclusions.* New York:

Macmillan. 1917. $ 2.75. "The Pan-Psychism of Samuel Butler", pp, 1-43. バトラーの思想に於ける個性 (individuality, personal identity, self etc.) の問題を主として取上げたもの。バトラーを論ずるといふよりは、むしろ筆者自身の観念哲学を述べるためにバトラーを引合ひにだしたと言つた方が適當である。

3. Murry, J. Middleton : *Aspects of Literature*. 1st ed., 1920. Travellers' Library ed., 1934. 3s. 6d. "Samuel Butler", pp. 120-34. 「萬人の道」を批評せる文章と H. F. Jones のバトラー傳を批評せる文章を結合したもの。ジャーナリズムの城を脱しない。

4. More, Paul Elmer : *A New England Group and Others*. Shelburne Essays xi. Boston & New York : Mifflin. 1921. $ 2.00. "Samuel Butler of Erewhon", pp. 167-99. バトラーの irony を主として取扱つた好論文。

5. Cunliffe, J. W.: *English Literature during the Last Half Century*. Macmillan. 2nd ed., 1922. 10s. Chap. iv, Samuel Butler (1835-1902), by Jefferson B. Fletcher, pp.

6. Cazamian, Madeleine L.: *Le Roman et les Idées en Angleterre : L'Influence de la Science* (1860-1890), Strasbourg : Librairie Istra. London : Milford. 1923. 20 fr. Chap. III, Samuel Butler, pp. 172-238.

7. Ishida, Kenji (ed.) : *Erewhon*. Kenkyusha English Classics. Tokyo : Kenkyusha. 1924. (現在は一冊二圓で分賣せられてある。)

8. Chevalley, Abel : *The Modern English Novel*. (Tr. by B. R. Redman.) New York: Knopf. 1925. $2.50. Chap. iv. Samuel Butler and his Influence, pp. 90-108. 小說家としてのバトラーを取扱った、短いが理解ある論文。

9. Kingsmill, Hugh : *After Puritanism*. 1st ed. 1929. Duckworth's Georgian Library. 1931. 5s. "Samuel Butler", pp. 57-107. バトラーの性格と思想とに關するよくまとまった論文。

10. Massingham, H. J. and Massingham, Hugh (ed.): *The Great Victorians*. Nicholson & Watson. 1932. 8s. 6d. "Samuel Butler", by H. C. O'Neill, pp. 107-19. 平凡。

11. MacCarthy, Desmond : *Criticism*. Putnam. 7s. 6d. "Samuel Butler", pp. 1–16.

これは雑誌 *Life and Letters* (Oct., 1931) から再錄された論文である。バトラーを個人的によく知つてゐた友人がバトラーの個人的特徴に就いて述べたもの。

12. 中野好夫：サミュエル・バトラーの「萬人の道」。英語英文學講座。新英米文學社。1933. 豫約出版物。Pp. 23.

これはその唯一例をあげるにとゞまる。この essay はバトラーの生誕百年を記念し、同時に *Letters between Samuel Butler and Miss E. M. A. Savage* (既出) の紹介を兼ねたもの。筆者はバトラーを分裂した性格と考へ、その分裂のために一方では精緻な無分別な適用のために、彼の活動に於ける善きものと惡しきものと時代の知惠を超越したものが生れたと考へてゐる。

13. *The Times Literary Supplement.* Dec. 7, 1935. "Samuel Butler", pp. 821–2. Leading article. 定期刊行物に載つた文献を擧げると夥しい數にのぼるであらうが、これはその唯一例をあげるにとゞまる。この essay はバトラーの子供らしいもの、子供らしいものと時代の知惠を超越したものが生れたと考へてゐる。參考すべき意見である。

14. Legouis, E. and Cazamian, L.: Histoire de la Littérature Anglaise. Paris: Hachette. 1924. 20 fr. English translation, by H. D. Irvine and W. A. MacInnes. Dent. 1926–7. 2 vols. 10s. 6d. each. New ed. revised. 2 vols in one. 1930. 18s. Revised and cheaper ed. 1933. 10 s. 6 d. "Samuel Butler", pp. 1265–71. 英文學史のなかでバトラーを取扱った一つの最もすぐれた見本としてこゝに擧げる。Cazamian 教授はバトラーを、その表面的な反抗の精神にもかゝはらず、根柢に於ては調停者であるとし、その點で例へばジョーと比べてもより國民的であり、從つて全くイギリス的なイギリス人であると考へてゐる。

# 文學科研究年報

言語と文學

第四輯

臺北帝國大學文政學部

# 基督教並びに佛教に現れたる極樂の觀念

アルンデル・デル・レー

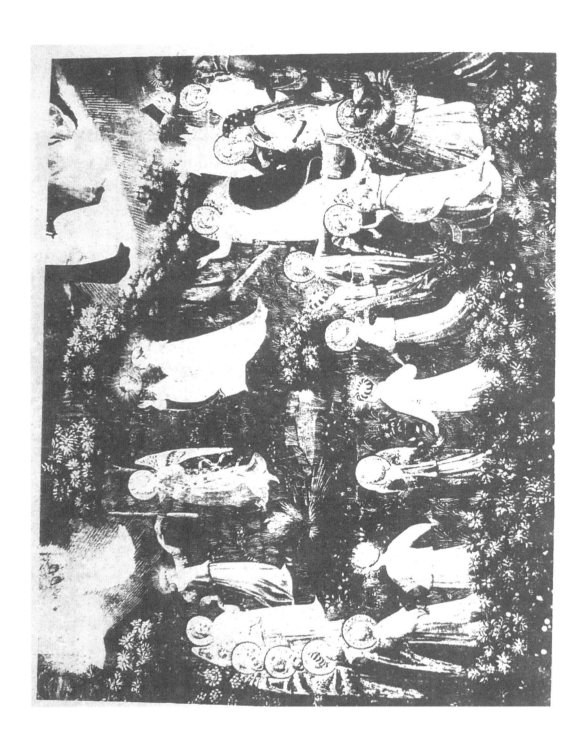

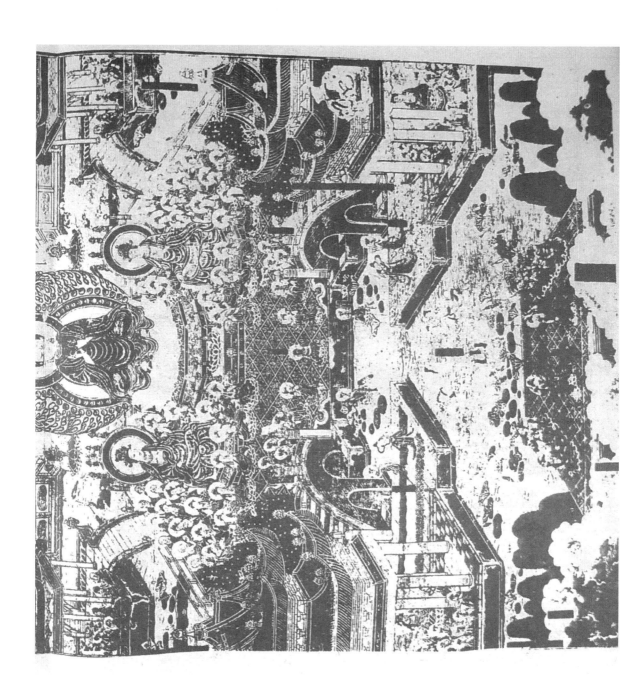

graph the luminous beauty of the scene nor the richness and purity of Angelico colouring which has perhaps never been surpassed. He was above all the painter of the felicities of heaven, as Ruskin said. "The notablest fulfilment of joy in him is that all nature becomes transfigured into the colours of blossoming....To Fra Angelico all nature becomes literally couleur de rose; so that architecture itself, trees, ground, all become rainbow-hued. The joy of his heart makes it like a crystal cut in the faith of the Trinity, and making all heaven's light seven-zoned."

---

Thanks are due to Messers. Alinari of Florence for the use of plates nos. 1, 2, 3, 4, 9 and to the British Museum for plates 5-8. I also desire to express my indebtedness to the Librarian of the Tokyo Imperial University Liberary for the generous loan of books.

type.... which has become stereotyped in Japan'. Date: IXth cent.

PLATE VIII. Paradise of Sakyamuni. (Tun-Hwang) According to Petrucci, (*Serindia*, p. 1410) the two Bodhissatvas, on each side of Sakyamuni are Akâsagarbha (Kokûzô), right and Kshitigarbha (Jizô), left. Of peculiar interest is the figure of the Buddha on the terrace in the foreground flanked by the same Bodhissatvas as above, save that Jizô here appears in monkish grab; his robe bears the red disk of the sun on the left shoulder and the white one of the moon on the right (with the tree of immortality) and, on the front, Mt. Meru with a man's figure on either side. It is thought that S. here is represented as an incarnation of B. as the liberator of souls and thus connects the mythical paradise with the East. (cp. *Avatamsaka sutra*) The elaborately decorated pavement on which the dancer is performing, and the heavenly mansions in the background should be noted. Among the paradises represented in these caves, the present one, while containing the usual characteristic features, is simple in composition as compared with the elaborate arrangement of the Taema-mandara type, of which hundreds of examples are found at Tun-Hwang, Date: probably contemporary to that of Pl. VII.

PLATE IX: Fra Angelico, Paradise, detail from Pl. I q. v. The scene might stand as an illustration for the lines from Sir Owayn, quoted (p. 65) The blessed and the angels are crowned with wreaths of flowers, the aureoles and the shining rays that encircle their heads is executed with gold leaf. It is impossible to convey in an ordinary photo-

and Man in the one case, between humanity, Amida and the Bodhissatvas in the other, although the latter never was expressed realistically as in the West, at least as regards representations of the 'pure land'.

PLATE VII: Paradise of Amida from the Grottoes of Tun-Hwang. British Museum, Aurel Stein Collection. Painting on silk, showing Amitâbha (Amida) with Avalokitesvara (Kwannon) on the right and Mahâsthama (Seishi) on the left, each with two attendant bodhissatvas. On either side of Amida are two pillars with a flaming jewel at the top, and two treasure trees supporting a canopy with floral scrolls. On each side of it two Apsaras are sweeping down. Canopies supported by similar trees may be seen over Kwannon and Seishi, but in this case they are many-tiered. At the back of the triad is a wall of multi-coloured marble blocks, below which is the lake on which swim ducks, emblems of happiness, and lotus buds containing infant souls. Above Amida are Buddhas seated on clouds, and figures of naked infants, representing reborn souls. On the terrace below the triad are Bodhissatvas and below other souls, as naked infants, and flaming jewels. According to Binyon, to whose descriptive account of this and the following plate I am indebted (v. *The Thousand Buddhas*, Ancient Buddhist Paintings from the Cave-Temples of Tung-Hwang, 1921, p. 21-22) the absence of celestial mansions and of the altar before the Buddha as in other such pictures of Paradise, as well as the composition, show that this is 'a specimen of Sukhavâtî scene developed independently of the orthodox

jewel in the lake of treasure, which emits an aureole of many coloured rays repeating in small the one which issues from the head of Amida, as described in the pure land sutras and in the Ojô Yôshu.

PLATE VI: Amida's Paradise, hanging scroll, now in the British Museum. A good example of the fully developed type of paradise *mandala,* surrounded by margins divided up into squares in which are represented scenes illustrating the miseries of the evil ways and the saving power of Amida. (cp. Pl. VII) The elaborate details follow closely those found in the sutras already mentioned. The figures of the central portion are traditionally Indian but the architecture of the buildings and their arrangement is Chinese, and there seems to be a strong Chinese influence in the marginal figures. Of particular beauty is the rain of flowers and musical instruments and the very elaborate grouping of the figures in the sky above Amida, which admirably convey the eager desire of the inhabitants of other pure lands and of countless Buddhas and Bodhissatvas to do homage and listen to Amida explaining the law in his land of Sukhâvatî. The present *mandala* seems to represent an intermediate stage between the classical Taema type and the developed frescos of the same type in the Grottoes of the Thousand Buddhas, and the purely Japanese ones of the 12th and 13th centuries. In this connection it is also worthy of notice that in Buddhist as in Christian art, (as a comparison with plates I-IV will show), there seems to be a somewhat parallel tendency to break down rigid iconographic traditions and to stress the human— divine relationship between Christ, the Church triumphant

LATE V: Amida's Paradise (upper portion), Japanese painting on hanging scroll, from the Genshôji (Osaka Higashi Kôzu) now in the British Museum. This is a good example of the development of the 'paradise' *mandara* in Japan, where the artist, partly perhaps under the influence of the less formal and stereotyped Jôdo and Shinshu Buddhism, tends to break away from the rigid symmetry and formal balance characteristic of the *mandara* from Central Asia. Raphael Petrucci in his excellent essay on the paintings found in the grottoes of Tun-Hwang, defines the *mandala* as a "peinture disposant, symmetriquement, mais en dehors de toute diagramme, un ensemble d'assistants autour d'un personnage central", and suggests that the *mandala* scheme goes back to the VII th-VIII th centuries, perhaps earlier, and is of importance as showing the influence of Bactria and Persia upon the development of Mahayana (Amidist) Buddhism which is most fully illustrated in central Asia. (Serindia, vol. iii, App. E, part III.) Unlike earlier works of this kind, other 'ways' of existence are introduced in to the lower portion—animals, demons, hungry ghosts and hells—the miseries of which are vividly treated to emphasize not merely the joys of Amida's 'pure land' as such, but the unique possibility of salvation it offers to all, whoever they may be. The saving power of the 'nembutsu' in this case is dramatically portrayed in the *raigô* procession which stretches across the scroll and divides or, perhaps better, links up the world of human being with paradise. The composition is remarkable for its flowing lines and the sense of rythmic movement which seems to pervade every corner of the scroll. Of particular interest is the magic

The realistic portraiture of the bottom central group is in sharp contrast with the idealized faces of the other blessed to whom, however, the painter has given an expression and pose suited to his or her character. It is also worth noting that, unlike what is generally the case at this date, Orcagna has dared to place the throne of Our Lady on a level with that of Christ.

PLATE IV: Paradise, by Benozzo Gozzoli, 1420-1497. Florentine school. Florence, Chapel of Palazzo Riccardi (c. 1459), left hand panel of recess. Ruskin draws attention to the orderly and symmetrical treatment of the landscape characteristic of the religious painters of the Quattrocento, who wished by this means to convey the spiritual nature of a world whence all signs of decay, disturbance or imperfection are banished. The details as well as the whole feeling of this and its corresponding panel admirably illustrate the descriptions of paradise given in the *Phœnix* and other early works, combined at the same time with unmistakable traces of humanistic influence, which contrast with the purely spiritual atmosphere of his master's (Fra Angelico) paradise (Pl. IX). The scene indeed, like that of Benozzo's great fresco of the Magi in the same chapel, is such as one may still see in the hills round Fiesole, near one of the Medici villas, and reflects the changed temper of an age for which—in the words of J.A. Symonds —"the cheerfulness of nature and the joy that comes to men from living in a many-colourd world of inexhaustible delight were sufficient sources of inspiration."

Our Lady(?) St. John the Baptist, a cherub, St. Peter and the (?) archangel Gabriel. At the back a cypress and three (!) palm-trees may be seen which have a symbolic meaning. The mosaic is remarkable for its colouring, beautiful design and excellent state of preservation and is of particular interest as showing a gradual but definite breaking away from the rigid iconographic tradition of the Byzantine school and the earliest stirrings of a new spirit in such eschatological compositions.

PLATE III: The glories of Paradise, by Andrea (di Cione) Orcagna, ? 1308-1368. Florentine school. Florence, church of Sta. Maria Novella, Strozzi Chapel (fresco). The angels, apostles, prophets, saints, martyrs and virgins are arranger symmetrically and hierarchically, on each side of the double throne on which sit Christ and Our Lady, interspersed with angels playing on various kinds of instruments, the second and third rows being occupied by the apostles and the patriarchs. In the two lowest tiers are the virgins and the holy women. Below the throne on a cloud are two angels, while two angels with long trumpets separate as it were the upper from the lower ranks of the blessed. In a kind of opening at the centre is a group of figures of men and women in contemporary dress, representing the latest arrivals among the company of heaven, while in the foreground on the right is an angel leading a women and a man to paradise, which rests upon a bank of clouds. The colours are glowing and the whole composition is of great decorative beauty. In composition, colouring and treatment of the subject, Orcagna occupies a place halfway between Giotto and Fra Angelico.

David and King Solomon. The nails, keys, bolts etc, that lie scattered under the feet of Christ symbolize the breaking asunder of the gates of hell and of the bonds of original sin and death which had held man captive. The lower part of the mosaic is divided into three horizontal bands, the lowest of which is divided into five compartments. In the centre of the upper band Christ sits enthroned between Our Lady (right) and St. John Evangelist (left), below him are two Cherubins, and between them two wheels symbolising the Ophanin. From the feet of Christ flows a stream of fire reaching down to hell. (cp. *Book of Enoch,* ed, vit. ch. xiv, 19, and *Daniel,* vii). The wheels referred to, however, may be those of the throne of God mentioned by the latter, loc. cit, 9. On each side of the triad are the apostles and behind them the ranks of those who had been sealed with the seal of God (*Rev.* vii, 3, ff). The band below represents the angels calling forth the dead who have perished in the sea (left) or have been devoured by wild beasts (right). The centre shows a throne on which lies the book 'sealed with seven seals' behind which rises a cross at each arm of which is a seraph. Two angels stand one on each side of the throne, before which the figures of a man and a woman are kneeling. (cp. *Rev.* v, 1 ff.) Above the lunette over the door enclosing a picture of the Mother of God, is an angel holding a pair of scales in which the good and bad deeds of man are weighed, and opposite him a group of demons; further to their left two angels are casting evil doers into the fires of hell. On the corresponding right hand upper compartment are the hierarchies of the saved and, immediately below, what appears to be a kind of garden or earthly paradise with(?) St. Joseph,

of S. Marco. The panel depicts the Last Judgment when all graves will be opened, man will resume his original body, sinners be cast into everlasting hell and the righteous enter heaven. In the upper part Christ appears seated in glory surrounded by the hierarchies of angels, flanked on the right by Our Lady and on the left by St. John the Evangelist. To right and left are the apostles, patriarchs, saints and martyrs amongst whom St. Dominic (extreme right) and St. Francis (extreme left). Immediately below, separated by two rows of opened graves, are the blessed (right) and the damned (left) whose rank and position in this life are shown by their dress. In the left hand corner is the abyss of hell the bottom of which is occupied by Lucifer, while the upper part is divided into seven compartments—one for each of the seven deadly sins. On the opposite corner angels are seen welcoming the saved souls and leading them to the shining gates of the Heavenly City, while others are dancing and singing with the blessed on the flower-besprent lawns of Paradise. (cp. pl. ix.)

PLATE II: The Day of Judgment. XIIth century mosaic, Byzantine school. Cathedral of Torcello (Venice). The upper part represents the First Resurrection. Christ is seen leading Adam out of Hell, and trampling upon Death. The female figure behind Adam seems to be Eve, while that on Christ's left is possibly St. John the Baptist who according to the Gospel of Nicodemus, announced to those in Hell the coming of Christ and their speedy liberation. The figures on the left, in the background represent the patriarchs of the Old Testament, while the two on the right may be King

ence; a state where God's beauty, power, majesty and love are made manifest in all their richness and the blessed live and move and have their being thus fulfilling the purpose for which Man was created and redeemed. If one were to try and sum up what above all else characterizes the most inspired pictures of the Christian Heaven and differentiates them from those of Amida's Paradise, one might say that it is the consciousness that perfect harmony and union between God and Man, as supremely expressed in the dual nature of Christ, has been finally realized and not that Man has ceased to be man.

As the Amida scrolls render admirably the Buddhist conception of paradise, so Orcagna and Fra Angelico render sensible to the beholder the feeling of the Christian heaven above described albeit in a somewhat different manner; the former bringing out the divine spirit in man, the latter transfiguring humanity. In the words of Ruskin: "....with Fra Angelico the glory of the countenance (v. pl. x) reaches to actual transfiguration; eyes that see no more darkly, incapable of all tears, foreheads flaming....with the writing of the Father's name upon them, lips tremulous with life, and crimson with the light of the coals of the altar—and all this loveliness, thus enthusiastic and ineffable yet sealed with the stability which the coming and going of ages as countless as sea-sand cannot dim nor wear, and bathed by an ever flowing river of holy thought, with God for its source, God for its shore, and God for its ocean." (*Hist. of Chr. Art,* 75)

PLATE I: The Last Judgment, by Beato (Fra Giovanni) Angelico, 1387-1455. Florentine school. Florence, Museum

East. The point just made seems to acquire even greater significance if we bear in mind the profound changes undergone by Buddhism in the course of its long history and its adaptability as well as the almost antithetical attitude towards life and death of the Japanese and the Indians.

Setting side by side the pictures of Sukhâvatî and those of Paradise, some illuminating differences between the spiritual atmosphere of the two paradises, apart from all details, at once become apparent. The former is a vision of a mythical land conjured up by and emanating from Amida modelled on the parks and gardens of some oriental potentate possessing magical powers and the imagination of a superman. It is a dream world, not a real one, yet paradoxically, it is just its non-existence outside the mind of Amida that makes it real and tangible to believers in him, and free it from all imperfections. Its features are therefore proper to a land where man, through the mysterious powers of Amida, enters and makes progress in the way of the Buddha. The artist has no need to make it appear convincing to human eyes while preserving its spiritual character. As a state it is supra-human, beyond mortality but also beyond humanity.

But if we turn now to the representations of Paradise illustrated in plates I, II, III—to which many other examples might be added—we become conscious immediately of the fact that heaven is not a dream-vision, a creation *ad hoc* (if so one may call it) such as was the Garden of Eden, but the abode of God, the Church Triumphant and the Angelic hierarchies; coeval with Him—since where He is there is heaven—created by Him outside of space and in an eternity beyond time, having Himself for its centre and circumfer-

from the artist'. Here we are, however, immediately faced with a difficutly that has an important bearing on the representation of paradise. While for the Christian the body is sinful by reason of its origin, through grace it is also 'the shrine of an indwelling spirit nobler than itself'; for the Buddhist, on the other hand, the body and all the components of what *appears* to (but does not) constitute an individual—since there is no permanent, separate ego—are the source of all evil and sorrow since they attach man to what is false, unreal and transitory. The vital importance of Amida's Pure Land lies in the fact that rebirth in it means not only a liberation from the temporal limitations and impurities of the body, but the realization of its *non-existence* as an objective reality. The souls of the Christian blessed, at least until the final resurrection, are clothed in purified and spiritual forms free from all imperfections, transhumanized but not superhuman or divine. The figures that people Sukhâvatî have only outwardly human form; they are not spiritual creatures with an individuality or a personal history, but more or less pure essences according to the degree in which they have realized their virtual Buddhanature. They are, in fact, a variation of the Buddha type of humanity which persists unchanged in all the paradise pictures from Central Asia to Japan with scarcely any change over a long period of centuries. Such a remarkable instance of unbroken iconographic tradition has no exact parallel in the West, as the plates clearly show in however limited a way, and is the result of religious beliefs quite as much as of artistic and technical conventions, powerfully determining factors though the latter be especially in the

## II.

## PLATES

NOTE: The selection of plates has necessarily been limited by considerations of a practical nature, and made with a view to giving, so far as possible, some idea of the arrangement and character of the Buddhist and Christian paradise, while showing at the same time the reciprocal interdependence of religious art and literature which derive their significance largely from a common belief in the afterlife. As John Addington Symonds admirably puts it in his *Renaissance in Italy* (vol. iii, Fine Arts, ch. 1, n. 1): "Religion is the universal poetry which all possess; and the artist, dealing with the mythology of his national belief, feels himself in vital sympathy with the imagination of the men for whom he works.... Painters are but the hands, and poets but the voices whereby people express their accumulated thoughts and permanent emotions....;around them floats the vital atmosphere of enthusiasms on which their own souls and the souls of their bretheren have been nourished."

The problem for the Christian as for the Buddhist artists who set themselves to portray paradise was—allowing for differences of attitude and belief concerning the ultimate significance of life—how to give pictorial form to an ideal world beyond the realm of sense and corporeity, in which the human body has no value in itself or for itself and ceases to be 'the true and adequate investiture of thoughts demanded

| | |
|---|---|
| B.C. 300–A.D. | (Hellenistic Period). Influence of Gk. upon Jewish eschatology. Contact of Greece with Persia and India. Formation of Greek-Jewish eschatological lit. in which previous elements mingle and develop. Further development of hell |
| A.D. 1–500 | (Hellenistic-Christian Period). Transformation of Greek-Jewish into Chr. eschatological lit. Romantic Jewish and Chr. use of Elysium ideal. Transformation and degradation of hell. |
| A.D. 1–1000 | Great and progressive elaboration of hell in Avestic, Sanskrit. Jewish and Chinese lit. Spread of Mahayana Buddhism in East and Central Asia. Development of Elysium ideal (Amitabha's Western Paradise) as substitute for that of heaven in Japan and China. |

## 600 A.D. — 1400 A.D.

| | IRELAND | ENGLAND | SCANDINAVIA |
|---|---|---|---|
| A.D. 600–700 | Earliest Irish escatological texts(?) purely Christian. | | |
| A.D. 700–800 | Irish non-Christian Elysium texts. Elysium: land to which mortals may penetrate by favour of gods, or the gods' land. No trace of heaven or hell. | Anglo-saxon version of Phoenix. | |
| A.D. 800–1100 | Romantic and didactic development of Irish Elysium. Christian transformation of it. (St. Brendan) | | |
| A.D. 800–1200 | | | Scand. eschatological texts. Heaven and hell clearly developed. Possible cosmological myth corresponding to Avestic Yima's grove. |
| A.D. 1200–1400 | Further Irish development in romantic, didactic and Chr. sense of Elysium ideal. | | Scand. romantic versions of voyage to Elysium. |

(f) *Growth of the Elysium conception among the Indo-Germanic races**

[This survey is based upon that given in Nutt (op. cit. i, p 326) with some additions, and arranged in tabular form.]

*B.C. 1500 — A.D. 600*

| | INDIA | PERSIA | GREECE |
|---|---|---|---|
| B.C. 1500–1000 | Vedic presentment of Yama's realm-golden age form of Elysium ideal developed into the heaven form. | | |
| B.C. 1000–800 | | | Homeric presentment of the gods' land and of realms to which mortals may be transported by special favour of the gods. |
| B.C. 1000–700 | Post-Vedic development of Yama's realm into a definite heaven, sometimes associated with him, sometimes with Indra. Elaboration of penal side of future life | | |
| B.C. 800–700 | | | Hesiodic account of golden age and of Elysium to which specially meritorious mortals penetrate after death. Development by later epic poets of Homeric Elysium. |
| B.C. 700–500 | | | Greek development of Elysium into heaven, coalescence of Elysium and gods' land. Elaboration of penal side of future life. |
| B.C. 500–300 | | | Elaboration and systematization of Gk. eschatology under influence of Orphic-Pythagorean doctrines. Romantic and didactic use of Elysium ideal in Utopia literature. |
| B.C. 600–A.D. 600 | Buddhist revolt in India against Brahminical eschatology. Romantic and epic use of heaven ideal. Romantic used of Elysium ideal | Avestic account of paradisiacal golden age, (Yima's realm) of cosmological Elysium (Yima's grove) in which human and animal life is stored up against world destruction. Elaboration of heaven, systematization and development of hell. | |

ing worms and serpents. The dead who attained eternal life were like the inhabitants of heaven, eat, drank and were dressed like them, but there is no mention of any heavenly city or of hierarchies of celestial beings. In fact the otherworld is a faithful reproduction of Egypt, each spirit living there the kind of life he lived upon earth. The domain of Osiris was reached by a ferry that sailed on the dark waters which come from the subterranean Nile and led to the great terrestrial ocean and its continuation in the sky, known also as the way of Osiris. Osiris, not unlike Yama, was formerly a celestial deity and later becomes the ruler of the underworld and it ssupreme judge and decides the fate of the dead.[8]

---

(8) (q. v. op. cit. Introd. lxviii-lxvi, and Max Muller, *Egyptian Mythology*, f. 176, 97.

held by certain Buddhist sects that the whole universe is an emanation of Buddha, with the identification of the individual with the gods, found in the Egyption religion, and used by the soul as a meaons of acquiring the necesaary power to overcome the monsters and dangers of the otherworld in the course of his pilgrimage to the throne of Osiris.

In the earliest times the Egyptian otherworld was supposed to be above the earth and was reached by a ladder. Subsequently, however, it was underground in the west or north west of Egypt, and approached through a gap in the mountains near Abdyos. The abode of the blessed dead in the XVIIIth Dynasty was called the 'Fields of Peace' where the deceased lived a life similar to that on earth. One section of it, known as the 'Field of Reeds', was represented like a large homestead or farm, intersected with canals. In the vignettes which illustrate the *Book of the Dead* the deceased may be seen sailing in a boat laden with offerings, or reaping wheat and driving the oxen which tread out the corn, or ploughing the land. The ideal of a future life is expressed by some of the prayers used in funeral ceremonies: "Let me be rewarded with thy fields, O God Hetep.... May I become a spirit therein, may I drink drink therein, may I plough therein, may I reap therein, may I fight therein, may I make love therein, may my words be mighty therein, may I never I be in a state of servitude therein, but may I have authority therein." In the same chapter (CX) the deceased addresses the gods of the various lakes of these Elysian fields and mentions having purified himself by bathing in the holy lake and having arrayed himself in the apparel of Ra. Amusements similar to those upon earth are provided such as snaring fowl and catch-

manent (incorrupted) in the deep house in the presence of Osiris, and thy *sahu* (spiritual body) becometh luminous among the living.... Thy nostrils inhale the sweet breath of Shu, thy nose breatheth the full breath of the north wind, gentle breezes and zephyrs refresh thy throat....thy words have power and vigour among the the spirits, thou eatest bread and thou imbibest ale, thy mapesty maketh its appearance in the form of a living soul.... Thou sailest through the air easily, thou hoverest in the shadow, and dost perform every act according to the dictates of thy heart. Thou risest in the sky and thy ,,hand is not separated therefrom, thou descendest into the Tuat and art not repulsed therefrom. Thou treadest the way of the gods of the horizon, and thou makest thy seat with the divine beings, of Amenti. Tou journeyst round the upper heaven in the following of the starry gods. Thou circlest about the night-sky face to face with their stars.....thou ministerest to those who are in the divine region of the earth. Thou travellest which ever way thou choosest.... Thou goest about in the Hall of the Maâti, thou approachest with the divine ministrants to see the Great God (Osiris), the divine beings who lead thee along to the holy place.... Thou fliest into the shrines of the house of the Gods of Tattu, thou wingest thy flight over the lands of Abdyos.... Thou betakest thyself to walk outside the House of gold, thou unitest thyself to the earth at the seat of the holy house, they duration of life is eternity, thy kingdom is everlastingness.... and thou renewest thyself for ever and ever.[7]

The above passages recall somewhat the powers and virtues enjoyed by the inhabitants of Amida's Western Paradise and by the Bodhissatvas. It is also worth comparing the conception

---

(7) (From *The Book of traversing Eternity*, reproduced in Wallis Budge's edn. of *The Book of The Dead* p. 679)

....See where, streaming forth radiance for thousands of
  miles,
Ever sits the compassionate Buddha, and smiles,
Giving joy to the victims of sorrow and strife
Who are saved by his law from the sorrows of life.
All his features of beauty no word can express,
For the sands of the Ganges in number are less;
Mark the flowers of the lotus encircling his seat
As if of themselves they sprang up round his feet.
Women would enter the home of the blest
In his innermost thoughts should incessantly rest
On that beautiful from like the clear moon on high
When the marches full-orbed through an unclouded sky.
By that halo of light that encircles his head,
On all living beings a radiance is shed.
The sun at noon-day is less glorious than he,
His compassion resembles a bottomless sea.
Without ceasing his arms are outstretched to relieve
The afflicted that weep, and the orphans that grieve,
For his mercy is such as none else can display,
And long ages of gratitude cannot repay.(6)

(e) *The Egyptian Happy Otherwerld.*

....Thy soul (that of the prophet of Amen-Ra) liveth in heaven in the presence of Ra, thy *ka* (double) acquireth the divine nature with the gods, thy body remaineth per-

---

(6) The above passages are taken from a Chinese collection of religious poems called *Tsing-tu-shî*, translated, somewhat freely, by Dr Edkins in his *Chinese Buddhism* (p. 172-74) The author was one of the patriarchs of the White Lotus in China and the founder of the Pure Land Guild.

The men of this world and the Devas of heaven,
And to each has the same wreath of glory been given.
The secrets of wisdom unveiled they behold,
And the soil that they tread on is bright yel low gold.
In that land of true pleasure the flowers never fade.
Each terraced ascent is of diamond and jade.
The law of Tathâgata sung by each bird
From thicket and grove in sweet music is heard.
The unwithering Upata, fairest of flowers,
Sheds fragrance around in those thrice lovely bowers.
There, each from the world that he governs, are found
Assembled in conference long and profound,
The ten supreme Buddhas who cease not to tell
The praise of the land where the genii dwell.
For there is no region so happy and blest,
As the heaven of great Amida far in the west.
On the moment of reaching it by new birth,
The material body of men while on earth
Is exchanged for another ethereal and bright,
That is seen from afar to be glowing with light.
Happy they who to that joyful region have gone!
In numberless *kalpas* their time floweth on.
Around are green woods, and above them clear skies,
Neither summer nor winter are ever there known
In the land of the Law and the Diamond Throne;
All errors corrected, all mysteries made clear,
Their rest is unbroken by care of by fear.
And the truth that before lay in darkness concealed
Like a gem without fracture or flaw is revealed.
. . . . . . . . . . . . . . . . .

'Hollow Hill' is describing his realm to Etain, the Celtic counterpart of Eurydice)

'Woman of the white skin, wilt thou come with me to the wonderland where reigns sweet-blended song; there primrose blossoms on the hair; snowfair the bodies from top to toe.

There, neither turmoil nor silence; white the teeth there, black the eyebrows; a delight of the eye th throng of our hosts; on every cheek the hue of the foxglove.

'Though fair the sight of Erin's plains, hardly will they seem so after you have once known the Great Plain.
the Great Land. A wonder of land, the land of which I

Heady to you the ale of Erin, but headier the ale of speak, no youth there grows to old age.

Streams gentle and sweet fow through that land, the choicest mead and wine. Handsome people without blemish; conception without sin, without crime.

We behold and are not beheld. The darkness produced by Adam's fall hides us from being numbered.

When thou comest, woman, to my strong folk, a crown shall deck thy brow—fresh swine's flesh and beer, new milk as a drink, shall be given thee my me, of white—skinned woman.'[5]

(d) *The Western Paradise of Amida*

(By Hwui-Yuen (Pap. E on), A.D. 370)

The pure land of the West, say what language can tell
Its beauty and majesty? There ever dwell

---

(5) Op. cit. p. 176. The story forms part of the famous work known as the *Book of the Dun Cow*.

### (c) *The Happy Otherworld of the Celts*

. . . . . . . . . . . . . . . .

There is a distant isle,
   Around which sea-horses glisten:
   A fair course against the white-swelling surge,—
   Four feet uphold it.

A delight of the eyes, a glorious range,
   Is the plain on which the hosts hold games:
   Coracle contends against chariot
   In southern Mag Findargat.

Feet of white bronze under it
   Glittering through beautiful ages.
   Lovely land throughout the world's age,
   On which the many blossoms drop.

An ancient tree there is with blossoms,
   On which birds call to the Hours.
   'Tis in harmony it is their wont
   To call together every Hour.

Splendours of every colour glisten
   Throughout the gentle—voiced plains.
   Joy is known, ranked around music,
   In Southern Mag Argatnél.

Unknown is wailing or treachery
   In the familiar cultivated land,
   There is nothing rough or harsh,
   But sweet music striking on the ear.

Without grief, without sorrow, without death,
   Without any sickness, without debility,
   That is the sign of Emain.... [4]

### (d) 'The Wooing of Etain'

(Mider, king of the mysterious Irish wonderland in the

---

[4] From. *The Voyage of Bran*, ed. cit. vol. I, pp. 4, 6.

who keep the garden, with never ceasing voices and blessed singing, they serve the Lord every day. And I said: 'What a very blessed place this is!' And those men spake unto me: (viii; 1-8)....This place, o Enoch, is prepared for the righteous who endure every kind of attack in their lives from those who afflict their souls: who turn away their eyes from unrighteousness, and accomplish a righteous judgment, and also give bread to the hungry, and clothe the maked, and raise the fallen, and assist the orphans who are oppressed, and who walk without blame before the face of the Lord, and serve him only. For them this place is prepared as an eternal inheritance. "(ix.)" And there shall be to them a great wall that cannot be broken down; and bright and incorruptible paradise shall be their protection, and their eternal habitation. For all corruptible things shall vanish, and there shall be eternal life." (lxi. 16) "I went out to the east, to the Paradise of Eden, where rest had been prepared for the just, and it was open to the third Heaven, and shut from this world. At the last coming they will lead forth Adam with our forefathers, and conduct them there, that they may rejoice, as a man calls those whom he loves to feast with him; and they having come with joy, hold converse, before the dwelling of that man, with joy awaiting his feast, the enjoyment and the immeasurable wealth and joy and merriment in the light, and eternal life." (xl ii. 3,5)

"Blessed are those who shall go the mansions of the blessed for in the evil one's there is no rest nor any means of return from them." (lxi. 3)[*3]

---

(3) Quoted from R.H. Charles, *A Critical History of the Doctrine of a future life.* 2nd. ed. London, 1913, p. 316—18.

writer gives rein to his imagination with scarcely veiled satyrical intent, thus placing the work in the category of fanciful descriptions of imaginary worlds and Utopias, of which Western literature has many examples (q. v. Paul Bloomfield *Imaginary Worlds*, London, 1932) and possesses an interesting analogue in *Wasōbiōye* (1774) by an anonymous Japanese writer (q. v. Chamberlain, Trs. As. Soc. Japan. vol. vii, 1879) which, later, inspired Bakin's *Musobiōye*.

(b) *The Paradise of the Third Heaven*

(From th *Book of the Secrets of Enoch* attributed to an Egyptian Jew of the first half of the 2nd. century A.D.)

"And these men took from thence, and brought me to the third Heaven, and placed me in the midst of a garden —a place such as never has been known for the goodliness of its appearance. And I saw all the trees of beautiful colours and their fruits ripe and fragrant and all kinds of food which they produced, springing up with delightful fragrance. And in the midst (there is) the tree of life, in that place on which God rests when he comes into Paradise. And this tree cannot be described for its excellence and sweet odour. And it is beautiful more than any created thing. And on all sides in appearance it is like gold and crimson and transparent as fire, and it covers every thing. From its root in the garden there go forth four streams which pour honey and milk, oil and wine, and are separated in four directions, and go about with a soft course. And they go down to the Paradise of Eden, between corruptibility and incorruptibility. And thence they go along the earth, and have a revolution in their circle like also the other elements. And there is another tree, an oil tree, always distilling oil. And there is no tree there without fruit, and every tree is blessed. And there are three hundred angels very glorious,

For them the sun shineth in his strength, in the world below, while here (in Elysium), tis night; and, in meadows red with roses, the space before their city is shaded by the incense tree, and is laden with golden fruits....

Some of them delight themselves with horses and with wrestling; others with draughts and with lyres; while beside them bloometh the fair flower of perfect bliss. And o'er that lovely land fragrance is ever shed, while they mingle all manner of incense with the far-shining fire on the altars of the gods.

From the other side sluggish streams of darksome night belch forth a boundless gloom.[2]

According to Josephus (*De Bello Judaico*, ii, 154-58), the Essenians sharing the belief of the "sons of Greece, maintain that for virtuous souls there is reserved an abode beyond the ocean, a place which is not oppressed by rain or snow or heat, but is refreshed by the ever gentle breath of the West wind coming in from the ocean; while they relegate base souls to a murky and tempestuous dungeon, big with never-ending punishment...."

This passage is a clear evidence of the spread of Platonic eschatological myths which, earlier through the Orphics and Neo—Platonism, influenced largely the conceptions of Paradise and Heaven as late as the XVIIth century, as may be seen in Dante, Spenser and, subsequently, the Cambridge Platonists, and has ever been a source of inspiration to poets (e.g. Shelley and Bridges).

But perhaps the best known description of these islands is that by Lucian (*True Story*, ii, 4 ff) in which the

---

(2) Pindar, 'Dirges', 95.

# APPENDICES

## I

## Additional Texts

(a) *Classical descriptions of the Abodes of the Blest*

....immediately after death, on earth, it is the lawless spirits that suffer punishment,—and the sins committed in this realm of Zeus are judged by One who passeth sentence stern and inevitable; while the good, having the sun shining for evermore, for equal nights and equal days, receive the boon of a life of lightened toil, not vexing the soil with the strength of their hands, no, nor the water of the sea, to gain a scanty livelihood; but, in the presence of the honoured gods, all who were wont to rejoice in the keeping of their oaths, share a life that knoweth no tears, while the others endure labour that none can look upon...But, whosoever, while dwelling in either world, hath thrice been courageous in keeping their souls pure from all deeds of wrong, pass by the highway of Zeus into the tower of Kronos, where the ocean breezes blow around the islands of the blest, and flowers of gold are blazing, some on the shore from radiant trees, while others the water fostereth; and with chaplets thereof they entwine their hands, and with crowns, according to the righteous counsels of Radamonthus, who shareth for evermore the judgments—seat of the almighty father, even the lord of Rhea with her throne exalted beyond all beside.[1]

---

(1) Pindar, 'Olympian Odes', ii, 59-77 trs. by Sandys, Loeb Library.

tween the *Ojô Yôshû* and the *Commedia* do not bear close examination, being based on external details alone. Of greater interest is Dr. Anezaki's parallel study of the Inferno and the vision of Mahamaugalayâna published in *Tôa no Hikari,* 1906, 1906, vol. i, n. 5, pp. 90-95

death into four troops, which appears to be peculiar to Irish writers: those who are not greatly bad, who go to hell after judgment; the very bad, who go to hell at once without adjudication; the good who are not greatly good, who after judgment go into their regard (e.g. King Cormac); the very good, who at once pass into heaven and receive their golden reward. Nutt, agrees with Prof. Zimmer in attributing the classification to the influence of the pre—Christian Celtic happy otherworld, which was intended as the resting place of those who were unworthy of immediate heavenly beatitude. To correspond with this temporary Elysium a provisional hell was added. (Nutt, *Voyage of Bran*, I. p. 225-6)

161) *Paradise Lost*, III, lines 349-371
162) v. pl. v, vi
163) The descriptions of the heavens, paradises, hells or other regions of the beyond can hardly be placed within the category of visions any more than such poems as the *Phoenix* or *Christ*, except when they do represent an individual experience.
164) *Jâtaka*, No. 511, (No. 84 of the *Licou Tou King*).
165) The copy in my possession states that it was written down in 1851 at Eikyû temple in Yamato, but presumably it is a recension of a much older work.
166) The copy I have is the *Kantokuden*, written in 1723.
167) q. v. de Visser, op. cit., vol. II, p. 673-74
168) cp. *Inferno*, I, 31 ff.
169) ibid. 61 ff. 112. ff; II, 49, ff.
170) ibid. III, 1 ff. 70 ff.
171) The comparison drawn by Reichshauer and others be-

day until he has expiated them, after which he will be reborn as Samantaraja. In the intervals he enjoys, like Cormac, all the pleasures and privileges of his kingly position. In *Tundalus*, as in the *Commedia*, those guilty of incontinence are placed immediately below the Earthly Paradise; moreover unlike what is the case in earlier visions, the travellers are required to undergo purification before being allowed to approach the beatific vision. cp. De Groot, *Les Fêtes Annuelles d' Emoui*, vol. I, p. 193.

157) ed. cit. 1980-92. The original text has been slightly modernized. cp. Ojô Yôshû, p. 54 ante.

158) As in the case of the sutras, special privileges are accorded to those who aid and protect religious orders.

159) Analogous privileges are enjoyed by the inhabitants of the Western Paradise.

160) From *Celtic Anthology*, by Grace Rhys, p. 47-48 It should be added here that the visions of Tundalus and of *Sir Owayn* are greatly influenced by pre-Christian Celtic myths of a happy otherworld, and show how Christianity adopted and adapted the earlier conceptions to its purpose. The description of Paradise and Heaven found in both these works and in others of the same kind (e.g. the *Vision of Adamnan* and the *Tidings of Doomsday*) present characteristics which reveal unmistakeably Celtic rather than Christian origins and are closely related to such works as the *Voyage of Bran* and the "Wooing of Etain" found in the *Book of the Dun Cow*. (q. v. Appendix 1 post, p. 129f.) In *Tundalus* we also find the division of the human race after

have. is theological and homiletic in character, and contains many disquisitions on dogmatic points concerning the state of the souls in the otherworld which frequently recall the *Paradiso*. It is not improbable that the author should have been influenced by the *Commedia* with which in view of his residence in Italy, the is likely to have been acquainted.

149) The distinction between hell and purgatory lies not so much in the gravity and greater painfulness of the punishments suffered in the former, as in the fact that while the souls suffer through the senses and through the knowledge that they have deprived themselves for evermore of the grace and glory of God—which realization exceeds by far any physical pain—those in purgatory instead have the ultimate hope of salvation, and their sufferings are not only alleviated by the prayers of the faithful, but also by weekly angelic visitations.

150) op. cit., supra, visio 19ma, p. 207 ff.

151) cp. vision of Andreas Salus, ante, p. 47 and the vision of Bishop Salvius. q. v. St. Gregory of Tours, *Hist. Franc.* vii. 1

152) cp. n. 103 ante.

153) cp. *Paradiso*, III, 88-90, IV, 34-36

154) cp. *Paradiso*, XXXIII, and the *Visio Wettini*, (verse) by Bishop Hetto. (Migne, *Patr. Lat.* CV, col. 762 ff.)

155) cp. *Paradiso*, IV, 28-42, and ante, p.

156) There are some remarkable resemblances between the legend of King Cormac and that of Yama, king of Hell who, on account of his sins when king Vaisali, has molten copper poured into his mouth three times a

141) loc. cit.; lines 73-78
142) cp. description of Heavenly Jerusalem, ante, p. 15. and that of Amida's Western Paradise, ante, p. 52 ff. It would seem, however, that the list of stones is here inserted, less for symbolic than for artistic purposes.
143) loc. cit. lines, 112-13, 115-20
144) ibid. lines 145-53, 157-62. (cp. ante, *Pilg. Prog.* p. 138 ff. The curtesy of the blessed is stressed by Dante and eariler in the Vision of St. Paul. cp. pl. i.
145) ibid. lines 187-92
146) ibid. lines 380-84.
147) The lilt and the phrasing of these lines recall the 'Ancient Mariner', and indeed the whole rendering whether deliberately or unconsciously, happily combine the music of the original with that of Coleridge.
148) *Visiones Georgii.* A.D. MCCCLIIII, ed. by. L.L. Hammerich (Historisk-filologiske Meddelser. xviii. 2, Copenhagen, 1931). The protagonist appears to have been a knight sent by the King of Hungary to Apulia to keep order in that province, during which time he had been guilty of much wanton cruelty and oppression. As in the case of Sir Owayn, he was struck suddenly with horror and terror at the thought of his sins, and fearing the wrath of God he put on pilgrim's garb and travelled to Ireland' where he obtained letters from the Bishop of Armagh granting him permission to enter St. Patricks Purgatory. His account of the visions seen in it were subsequently duly attested by letters from the Bishop of Armagh and the Prior of Lough Derg. This record which is oné of the most complete we

Lough Dergh in Co. Donegal. As late as the XVIIIth cent. the place was visited by numbers of pilgrims from all countries, some of whom dared to face the horrors of the Purgatory and afterwards left accounts of what they saw there.

138) Sir Owayn lived in the reign of King Stephen (1135-54). After having served his sovereign for many years, he returned to Ireland his native land. Seized with sudden remorse at the thought of the countless sins committed he went to the Bishop of Armagh and declared his intention of entering the Purg. of St. Patrick, in order to expiate his crimes. The Bishop sent him to the Prior of Lough Derg, and having fulfilled all the requirements and performed the prescribed ritual, he was shriven and solemnly led to the entrance to the cavern where he was told he would meet God's messenger who would instruct him as to what he should do.

139) q. v. note 129 above.

140) The final trial of the narrow bridge is found in many visions, e.g. that of Furseus (St. Forsey) recorded by Bede in *Hist. Ecclesiastica* (iii. 19) and that of a monk of Wenlok Abbey told by Boniface in one of his epistles to the Abbess Eadburga. Mention is also made of it in The Dialogues of Gregory the Great (iv 36). Analogues are found in the Taoist hell, in Mazdean (the bridge Cinvat) and in Norse mythology (Bifröst). In Tundalus, however, the bridge is encountered earlier during the passage through hell and is two miles in length and crosses a lake full of horrible monsters. (q. v. ed. cit. lines 501 ff.)

from the *Wooing of Etain* afford examples of the two types. The first type is connected with the genre of story—telling known as *imrama* or 'Oversea Voyage Literature' of which the most famous Christian example is the *Navigatio Sancti Brendani*, translated into most European languages, and included in Caxton's Golden Legend (Temple Classics, vol. vii, p. 48). A Christian example of the second type is the story of the priest Elidurus, reported by Giraldus Cambrensis (Gerald du Barri), who was taken by fairy folk throught a subterranean passage to a delightfull land whose people lived on milk and saffron, swore no oaths and despised human ambition and inconstancy. A full account of such Celtic legends is given by Alfred Nutt in his 'Essay upon the Irish vision of the Happy Otherworld and the Celtic doctrine of Rebirth,' appended to Kuno Meyer's edition of the *Voyage of Bran*, London, 1895, 2 vols, to whom I am indebted for the information given above.

135) e.g. *Sir Gawayne and the Green Knight*, *Sir Orpheo*.

136) It should be noted that in *Sir Owayn* as in the *Commedia*, the hero penetrates directly into the other world in his own body, while in others (sc. *Tundalus*) the body lies in a cataleptic state while the vision lasts, the soul alone experiencing the tortures of hell (in some cases) and the joys of heaven.

137) Among the earliest accounts of the famous sanctuary is that given by Giraldus Cambrensis in *Topographia Hibernica* (1187) who situated it upon one of the twin islands in a lake in Ulster, afterwards identified as

soul in heaven and the physical constitution of the Heavenly City, recognizes two kinds of vision: one, like that of St. Paul, in which the 'theolept' is ravished out of the body, and the other in which the initiate perceives the truth through contemplation, and concluded that the study of such visions would bring with it wisdom.

132) Pindar, Olymp. ii, 53 ff., e.g. *Odyssey* (Bk. XI), *Aeneid* (Bk. VI), *Somnium Scipionis, Gylfaginning, Voluspó* etc.

133) q. v. supra, n. 21 and, post, Appendix I (c) The voyage of Bran.

134) e.g. The voyages of Gorm recounted in Saxo Grammaticus. Celtic mythology abounds in legends of this kind dealing with journeys to the happy otherworld. These belong to two types—the 'Oversea' and the 'Hollow Hill' type. "In the former the magic land lies across the Western main, it is marked by every form of natural beauty, it possesses every sort of natural riches, abundance of animals, of fish, of birds, of fruit: its inhabitants are beauteous, joyful; a porttion of the land is dwelt in by women alone; all earthly ills, both physical and moral are absent; in especial age brings neither decay, nor death, nor diminution of the joy of life; love brigs neither strife, nor satiety nor remorse. ....Time passes there with supernatural rapidity, the mortal who once penetrated there may not return unscathed to earth." In the 'Hollow' type the wonderland lies with in the fairy hills (*sid*). The passages quoted (Appendix I) from the *Voyage of Bran* and

well as 13 French MSS. amongst which the well-known one by Marie de France, and others in Italian. For a study of the work, v. T. Wright, *St. Patrick's Purgatory* (1844) and the more recent *L'autre Monde*, Mythes et Légendes, by Philippe de Félice (Le purgatoire de Saint Patrice), Paris, 1906, to which I am greatly indebted.

130) Many early MSS. of the work are extant, in Latin, French, German, Italian and Norse. According to the prologue it was composed in 1149. Among modern recensions one of the most important is the composite one edited by Wagner (Halle), based upon the M. E. text, which I have used in conjunction with the Lat. text given in Migne (*Patr. Lat.* CCXIII, col. 1038 ff.)

131) q. v. J.E. Wells, *A Manual of Writings in M. E.* 1050-1400, for bibliographical notes on works of this nature (ch. V. d. pass.), E. J. Becker's *A Contribution to the comprehensive study of Med. Visions of Heaven and Hell* (Baltimore, 1899), Friztsche, *Die Lat. Vis. des Mittelalters*, in 'Romanische Forschungen' (ii, iv), Routh, *God, Man and Epic Poetry* (vol. ii, Med.) 1927, D'Ancona, *I precursori di Dante*, Karl Vossler, *La Divina Commedia* (vol. ii, pt. I) and other special or general studies in various languages. Wells, op. cit., points out the special use of the term 'vision' in the case of Sir Owyan, Dante and St. Paul, who do not merely have a vision of the otherworld, but visit it in person. In this connection it may be added that Richard Rolle of Hampole in part VII of the *Pricke of Conscience* (c. 1350) when describing the life of the

wise.

127) cf. Fritzsche, *Die Persische Lehre von Jenseits und Jüngsten Gericht*. (Jahrbücher für protestant Theologie, 5er Jahrgang, Leipzig, 1877) who suggests that these mediaeval Christian eschatologists were influenced by ancient Persian mythology. The subject is dealt with exhaustively by Dr. N. Söderblom (op. cit.)

128) Moses Bar-Cephas, in his *Commentaria de Paradiso* (Migne, *Patr. Gr.* CXI, col. 488) observes that in reality there is only one paradise which has two aspects—a corporeal and an incorporeal one. While the former possesses all the characteristics of the Earthly Paradise, the latter instead is a state rather than a place, in which the souls enjoy a temporal and holy life devoted to meditation of divine as well as created things and creatures —not unlike the nirvana 'in this life' found in Buddhism. Those who live in such a paradise live indeed a blessed and angelic life illuminated by the rays of the Divine Knowledge. And just as earthly food nourishes the body, so the thought of God himself and of his creation nourishes the soul.

129) A number of English versions of the work are in existence, e.g. that contained in the *South-English Legendary or Festival* (in verse), from MS. Laud 108 (Bodl. Lib.) edited by Dr. Carl Horstmann (E.E.T.S.) The passages quoted are from Miss Weston's modernized version of the M.E. text (MS. Auchinleck, Advoc. Lib. Edinburgh) published in her *Chief Middle English Poets*, cit. supra. The original Latin account is attributed to Henry of Saltrey, but there are several others, as

121) cp. the vision of Andreas Salus, ante, p. 46
122) *Ojo Yôshû*, ch. ii, p. 70
123) cp. *Tundalus*, post, p. 73
124) The grotto-temples of Tun Hwang with their marvellous frescoes the greater part of which portray Amida's and other paradises (q. v. Mission Pelliot, *Les grottes de Touen-Houang*, Paris, Geuthner), and the rich collection of paintings brought from there by Sir Aurel Stein, and now in the British Museum (v. pl. vii).
125) The matter has been discussed very widely, q. v. for instance the very illuminating article on 'Enlightenment and Ignorance' by Dr. T. Suzuki in *Eastern Buddhist*, vol. iii, n. 1, p. 1 ff.
126) So far as Indian aesthetics are concerned, the subject has been admirably dealt with by Dr. Heimann (op. cit. ch. 6, p. 96 ff.). Many of her remarks are applicable equally to Japanese Buddhist art, as may be seen from the following quotation"....external form is of but secondary importance. It is therefore the psychological impression, associating the artefact itself with some general ideas, that really counts....nothing ever stands alone; everything is in one way or another typical, and is consequently a recognized truth that can be thrown into the briefest aphoristic form; here again the single expression is the representative of the whole." (loc. cit. pp. 104, 105) If by 'external form' above, we understand the subject or content of the artefact in itself, with no reference to technique, the statements seem to sum up what are, in effect, two of the outstanding characteristics of Japanese art, religious or other-

resse j'ai gagné ce paradis et mon bonheur dépasse toute description."' La dama répondit: 'Si elle m'apparait à moi aussi, je croirai ce que tu me dis.' Dans la nuit suivante la morte lui apparut en effet et la salua avec respect. 'Parviendrai-je,' lui demanda la dame, 'moi un jour dans le pays du bonheur?' 'oui,' répondit-elle, 'tu n'as pas besoin qu'à suivre ta servante.' En reve la dame suivit sa servante et vit bientôt un lac immense couvert d'innombrables lotus rouges et blancs en différents états, les uns en fleur, les autres fanés. Elle demanda ce que les fleurs signifiaient. La fille répondit: 'Ce sont des âmes humaines dont, sur terre, les pensées étaient dirigées vers l'endroit du bonheur. Le premier désir du paradis d'Amita fait naître une fleur dans le lac céleste et elle grandit et embellit de jour en jour, tant que la justice de la personne qu'elle represente, fait des progrès; en cas contraire elle perd sa splendeur et se flétrit.' La dame demanda le nom d'une fleur brillante qui était toute enveloppée de splendeur et qui rayonnait merveilleusement. 'Ta servante' dit Yankie. Puis elle demanda le nom d'une autre fleur et eut la réponse: 'C'est Mahu'. La dame continua: 'Où est-ce que je renaîtrai moi?' Alors l'âme bienheureuse la conduisit plus loin et lui montra une hauteur qui rayonnait d'or et d'azur. 'Voici' dit-ellae,' ta demeure futuree. Tu seras une des premières au rang des bienheureux.' Lorsque la dame s'éveilla elle demanda Yankie et Mahu (les deux domestiques). La première était encore parmi les vivants. C'est ainsi que la dame apprit qu'une âme qui avance en sainteté et qui persévère, demeure déjà au pays du bonheur, quand même son corps séjourne encore dans ce monde périssable.

116) *Ojô Yôshû*, trs. cit., p. 76. The details mentioned are not found in the three sutras above.

117) No description of these lakes is given in LSV, but v. KW. 13, p. 174.

118) v. ppl. v, vi

119) KW. 19, p. 181 ff. It should be noted that while close in essentials, details differ somewhat in LSV, SSV., and KW; e.g. SSV. does not give a minute description of the gem trees, while stress is laid instead on the walls surrounding Sukhâvatî. Considerable differences are also found in the list of gems. q. v. note 3 to st. 3 of SSV., p. 92-93 cp. the *Ratna-kûta-dharma paryâya* (Paripriccha) treatises on Paradise (q. v. pl. ii)

120) op. cit. ch. ii, p. 70 As regards conditions of rebirth v. KW., p. 188 ff. Grunwedel in *Mythologie du Buddhisme au Tibet et en Mongolie* (pp. 119-20), quotes a charming legend of supposedly Chinese origin, relating to rebirth in the Western Paradise, trs. by Schott in: *Über den Buddhismus in China und Hochasien,* which admirably illustrates the influence that this belief had upon the people:—

> Du temps de la Dynastie Sun une vielle femme pieuse et ses deux domestiques ne vivaient que pour le 'pays du bonheur' (Sukhâvatî). Un jour l'une de ces jeunes filles dit à sa camarade: 'cette nuit je passerai au paradis d'Amita.' Dans cette même nuit un parfum balsamique remplit la maison et la fille mourut sans avoir été malade auparavant. Le lendemain celle qui survivait dit à la dame: 'Hier la morte m'apparut dans un rêve et me dit. "Grace aux exhortations perpetuelles de notre mait-

ferable to that of all the other Buddhist heavens. For the merits of this Bodhissatva v. also *Ojô Yôshû*, ch. vii, p. 84-85. see also Appendix I, quotations from Hwui-Yuen's hymn to the Western Paradise.

106) *Amidakyô*, ed. cit. p. 91, st. 3 subsequently referred to as SSV. Sukhâvatî is the result of the vows made by Sakyamuni when he was the mank Dharmakara. The latter vary somewhat from those found in the LSV (*Larger Sukhâvatîvyûha*) in that rebirth in S. is promised to all, without exception, who remember and repeat even twice the name of the Buddha Amitabha, but that accumulation of a 'stock of merit' (good deeds) is essential to salvation is specifically denied. In the KW. (*Kwangyô*) the scheme of salvation is worked out in detail, in which the period elapsing between death and the opening of the lotus in paradise, varies in length according to the merits of the individual, with, however affecting the validity of the 'original' vow.

107) LSV. 9, st. 5-8, p. 23
108) LSV. 22, p. 43
109) LSV. 15, p. 23
110) LSV. 16, p. 33
111) cp. the trees that encircle the upper slopes of the mountain of the Garden of Eden in *Parad. Lost*. referred to above in n. 87.
112) KW. 10, p. 171
112) KW. 14, p. 175. cp. also quotation from *Tundalus* p. 72 post.
114) KW. 12, p. 172-73
115) LSV. 18, p. 38

Amida's paradise is one of many, establishes a fundamental distinction between it and the Christian paradise, quite apart from any similarities previously pointed out. Nevertheless, so far as the purposes of the present study are concerned, it should be regarded as a region more-nearly approximating to the Christian paradise described by Mediaeval artists and writers. For a comprehensive account of the various 'Pure Lands' v. *Hôbôgirin*, IIIème fasc., s. v. *butsudo*. Properly speaking, the Paradise of Maitreya stands in a class to itself since it is not of the otherworld but of this and to be realized many years hence, in a kind of millenium when humanity will be pure and faithful. According to the descriptions (q. v. B. Matsumoto, *Miroku Jôdo-rôn*, 1911) it is flat, fertile with many cities so close to one another that one can hear the cocks crow and the dogs bark. Its one great city—Tch'e-t'eou-ino, contains the seven jewels of the Wheel Kings, and life there lasts 84.000 years and in not subject to the three infirmities. Maitreya promises various benefits to those who call upon him, think of him or honour him; the latter will see him at the hour of death coming to meet them accompanied by all the gods, under a rain of mandarava flowers, and will be immediately reborn into the Tusita heaven where he is awaiting the day when he will become the last Buddha. It seems tolerably certain that the Paradise of Maitreya represents an intermediate stage between the earlier Bud. conception and the Amidist one of Paradise, but unlike the latter, it does not save mortals from rebirth, although it is a state pre-

Other accounts are found in the *Ab.-kósa* and in the *Yogâcârya-bhùmi-sastra*. As regards the former city, it is worth nothing that the floor of the Heaven of the 33 Gods is of a hundred colours and soft as cotton, while that of Sukhâvatî is of lapis-lazuli (*Kwangyô*) or golden (*Amidakyô*). For full description of the former (Hindu, *Svarga*) v. Beal, op. cit. p. 95 ff. It is interesting to compare such elaborate descriptions of heaven with the following invocation to the divine plant Soma in the IXth book of the *Rig Veda*:

> "Wherein is uncreated light, therein are placed world and sun, thither bear me Soma, where is the never-ending world of deathlessness.
> Where Vivasant's son (Yama) is king, in the firm vault of Heaven, where running waters are, there let me be undying.
> Where one moves at will, in the threefold firmament, in the threefold heaven of heavens, where the worlds of light are, there let me never dying.
> Where desire and fulfilment (are one) in the red space of heaven, where the ghostly food is, there let me be immortal.
> Where joy and delight, pleasure and satisfaction await, where desires are fulfilled, there let me be never dying." (Oldenberg's trs.)

104) This is natural since Bud. is a religion lived in direct and close contact with nature, actually as well as figuratively, and that the scenes of Sakyamuni's greatest discourses were laid in parks, gardens or in the mountain forests.

105) The fact that, however superior it may be in practice,

Indies—and his monks, as well as through traders, Christianity is known to have penetrated these regions, it is not unreasonable to assume (as in the case of Nestorianism and Manichaeism) that Christian and Jewish eschatological ideas may have in some measure coloured or influenced the beliefs of the peoples amongst whom they circulated as well as their representations of the heavenly regions. cp. post, Appendix I (b).

95) *Baralam and Yewasef*, ed. cit. vol. ii, p. 209-10
96) cp. Asvagosha's *Buddhakarita* (S.B.E. vol. XLIX, Bk. v, vv. 47-65, Bigandet, *Legend of the Burmese Buddha*, p. 61, also the Singhalese account (Spence Hardy, *Manual of Buddhism*, Legends, vii, p. 157), and that given in the introduction to the *Jâtaka*, vol. I, 58. The passage previously quoted is a good example of how the adapter has superimposed Christian ideas on to the original so as to bring it into line with Christian beliefs.
97) S.B.E. vol. xi
98) e.g. *Muryôjukyô*, ed. cit. sect. 22, p. 43
99) cp. *Vishnu Purâna, Agonkyô, Kusharon (Abhidharmakósa-'sâstra)*
100) *Journal des Savants*, 1831, p. 669
101) An interesting parallel is afforded by the *Paradiso* c. XXX.
102) Burnouf, *Introduction à l'Historie du Buddhisme Indien*, p. 556
103) e.g. description of the pleasure gardens, palace and jewelled city of Sudarsana, the abode of King Sakra (Indra), with its four parks and magic tree; and also of the city of Kusâvâti in the *Mahâsudassana Sutta*

Christianity in order to discredit the latter.

94) The original of this very popular work is attributed to St. John Damascene who wrote it down in Greek. Re search has shown the existence of a number of earlier versions in Arabic and Pehlevi believed to be the sources of the Christianized versions of the Buddha story, deriving from one or more recensions of the original composed in some Indian language by Buddhist propagandists either immediately before or immediately after the beginning of the Christian Era. The latest redaction (7th-8th cent.) is remarkable for the skilful manner in which the Indian atmosphere has been preserved while treating the essential facts in a manner acceptable to every Christian ascetic. For a full treatment of these and allied questions v. Wallis Budge, *Baralam and Yewasef*, Ethiopic version of the Christianized recension of the Buddhist legend of the Buddha and the Bodhisattva, vol. ii, Introduction. All other considerations apart, the diffusion of the legend is of importance as proving the existence of intercourse between the East and the West which, in the days of the Emperor Asoka, was not limited to trade. At the beginning of the Christian Era it would seem that Chinese in the East as well as Egyptians and Syrians in the West, were well acquainted with the parables and fables used by the Master in his teachings. Before the close of the VIth cent. according to Budge, Buddhism was preached in Parthia and neighbouring countries and many of the Sacred Books were translated into Pehlevi. Conversely, since through St. Thomas—the Apostle of the

ed.), Bari, p. 517 ff. De L., following up a suggestion made him by the noted German Buddhist scholar Eugene Neumann, relates the lines (*Paradiso*, xix, 70-75) to D's previous reference to the Ganges (*Par.* xi, 51) as a symbol of the East, pointing out that St. Francis, not only may be considered as the type of sanctity most closely approximating that found in the East (contemplative) in contradistinction to the Western (active) type personified in St. Dominic, but that, in effect, St. Francis of all Christian saints, was the one who most closely approached the Buddhist ideal. This leads him to suggest that D., like Petrarca, knew something about the gymnosophists and, possibly through the Legend of Barlaam and Joasaphat, also about Buddha. Furnthermore his almost certain acquaintance with the Travels of Marco Polo, that circulated in MS. in Florence and throughout Italy before 1307 in wihch, as is known, specific mention is made of Sakyamuni, seem to warrant the supposition that D. had Buddha in mind. The original text of the Travels was dictated by Marco Polo to Rusticiano da Pisa in 1298, while lying in a Genoese prison, and was written down in Venetianized French. The first printed edition (Italian) appeared in 1559, and the first English trs. in 1625. The hypothesis is an attractive one, but should be accepted with considerable reservations as indeed many other statements in the course of the book which unduly stresses the analogies between the alleged pessimism of Buddhism and that of Schopenhauer, and loses no opportunity—whether legitimate or otherwise—to compare Buddhism with

Christ', hence his nickname of 'Salus' (*stultus*), and died in the odour of sanctity about the middle of the Xth Cent.

90) The identification of birds with angels—easily understandable on account of their wings—in paintings and sculptures cherubs are represented as birds with human faces—is found in many of these visions. q. v. ppl. i, ii, iv.

91) cp. *Purgatorio*, XXVIII, 1-42.

92) In this and other visions (e.g. Sir Owayn, George of Hungary etc.) great attention is paid to the dress of the inhabitants of the heavenly regions. No where, however, has it been given greater prominence than in the Visions of Hildegarde of Bingen (XIIth cent. q. v. Migne, Patrol. Lat. CXCVII) who explains that the gold, gems and other ornaments with which the virgins of her visions were decked out, were to be understood symbolically not realistically, and that the bliss of heaven con only be shown in allegories since it surpasses the understanding of mortal men, thus adapting to her pur pose the classical argument of earlier writers. (cp. Taylor, op. cit. ch. xx, p. 472) It should be observed that as the visions become more elaborate and sensually realistic, and the puritanical reaction sets in, it was found desirable to justify such extravagances of the imagination as conceits possessing religious significance. (q. v. Toffanin, *La Fine dell'Umanesimo*, ch, xvi. and the studies of Benedetto Croce, Mario Praz and others on the influence of 'Secentismo' upon religious works.)

93) cp. G. de Lorenzo, *India e Buddhismo Antico* (Vth

region granted as an inheritance to the Ten Tribes of Israel, the inhabitants of which.

> '....want neither gold nor silver, neither eat flesh nor drink wine, but feed on honey and drink of the dew,....the water we drink is not from springs, but from the leaves to trees growing in the gardens....Neither do we ever wear garments made by the hand of men; nor is a word of lying heard in our land. No man marries two wives, neither doe the women dwell with us, they neither corrupt us nor we them; and when the wind blows, we smell through it the smell of gardens. In our land there is neither summer nor winter, neither cold nor hoar-frost; but on the contrary, a breath of life.'
> (Quoted in Nutt, *The Voyage of Bran*, vol. 1, The Happy otherworld, London, 1895, p. 251.)

86) cp. Vision of George of Hungary, post p. 67 ff.
87) cp. description of Eden in *Par. Lost*, Bk. iv, 130 ff.
88) The passages quoted in Dr. Gordon's trs. previously referred of A-S. texts, p. 266-67 are of Cynewulf's re-handling of the original. The insistence upon the absence of sorrow, sickness and death, should be noted and leads one to suggest that the beatitude of Paradise was largely conceived in negative terms, and that life was recognized as an evil not less strongly by Cristians than by Buddhists.
89) Migne, *Patrol. Graeca*, CXI, col. 663-670. Andreas was born in 880 A.D. and lived as a slave in Constantinople c. 890. In 910, according to some authorities, he began to simulate madness 'for the sake of

77) The difference between the two conceptions of blessedness previously alluded to—the paradisal and the heavenly—is of vital importance for Christianity as well as for Buddhism. It seems to suggest that in the former, an attempt is made to adapt religion so as to reconcile the practical temper with the spiritual needs of the times, by establishing a more rational human balance between the physical and spiritual worlds.

78) *The Questions of King Milinda* (Milinda Pañha), Part. II, trs. by Rhys Davids. S.B.E. vol. xxxvi, p. 211-12. It is interesting to compare Nagasena's detailed allegory of the City of Righteouness, with Hugo of St. Victor's allegorical explanation of the Heavenly Jerusalem in *De Claustro Animae*, Lib. iv, cap. xx-xlvii. (Migne, *Patrol.* CLXXVI, col. 1159-1182)

79) loc. cit. above, p. 213

80) i.e. right conduct, meditation, knowledge, emancipation, insight, discrimination, the jewel of seven-fold wisdom.

81) *Milinda,* p. 231-32

82) loc. cit. p. 191-92

83) loc. cit. p. 202-204

84) *Genesis,* VI, 4; q. v. also *Book of Enoch* (cit.) Sec. ii, ch. lxix. 4,5., p. 137

85) *Apocalypse of Peter,* v. 15 ff. translated by Adolphe Lods in *L'Evangile et l'Apocalypse de Pierre,* Paris, 1893, p. 86 ff. According to L. the text was composed before the middle of the 2 Cent. A.D., and was included among the canonical books until the 4th C. cp. also the *Christian Oracula Sybillina* and the Ethiopic *Conflict of Mathew.* The latter describes the blessed

the return of the procession along the 'Bridge of Death' (which extends the whole length of the village street), as the sun sets behind the Yamato hills, to the temple which represents the Land of Bliss. Dai-Seishi, bearing the image of Chûjôhimé—now become *hotoké*—enthroned upon the Lotus, leads the procession, dancing in exquisite triumph along the Bridge and through the rainbow tri-coloured curtains, which hang from poles surmounted by dragons' heads, into the temple over whose portal is a large *Rimbô*-Wheel of the Law flanked by two svastikas. A band of angelic musicians and a choir of monks welcome them as they enter."

The description is particularly interesting as being—in a sense—that of physical realization of the *raigô* idea which plays so important a part in Amidism.

76) I see abbove nn. 13, 14. It is difficult to see why the pursuit of nirvana should be considered as constituting one of the most important and essential differences between Hinayana and Mahayana, even granting that the latter, and in particular the Amidist sects, make the Western Paradise the immediate goal. As regards the theory of transference of merit, upon which so much stress is laid, this is not unknown to Hinayana, and the average Amidist believer, from a practical point of view is not really more unselfish than his Hinayanist counterpart, unless indeed one is prepared to accept the somewhat dangerous theory that, all things being equal, contemplation is inferior to action, in spiritual matters.

and has come to be considered an incarnation of Kwannon. The procession which enacts the coming of Amida with Twentyfive Bodhissatvas and the whole company of 'Heavenly men, women and children to compensate this little nun who—in her mortal life—was so grievously afflicted', is thus described:—

"Nothing can exceed the grace and tenderness of the rythmic dancing of Dai Seishi, 'The Mightiest One', who clad in emerald green, bears a large Lotus—blossom along the 'Bridge of Death' to receive the soul of Chûjô—himé at the Dai-Niô-mon which separates the Earth life from the Heavenly. At this great gate the *mikôshi* (coffin) with her corpse awaits Dai-Seishi's arrival, attended by a priest (also in emerald green) burning incense and carried by four white-robed bearers....Kôkôzu with a long crook holds a canopy over Seishi's head....Immediately behind Seishi comes Kwannon....Last of all comes Amida himself—the chief function of Mercy being to redeem others. All these are intent on welcoming this precious soul into Paradise. With them are the Twentyfive Bodishissatvas wearing immense halos and golden masks, each of whom has a singularly beautiful expression. They carry harp, guitar (*kôtô, biwa*) and drums on which the 'three Commas' (*mitsu domoe*) are painted....All exult in an ecstasy of joy at this divine comedy into which earth's tragedy has been transformed. The church on earth is represented by the highest dignitaries of the neighbouring monasteries, arrayed in most gorgeous vestments. Crimson umbrellas are held over them. Thousands of simple peasants await in breathless silence and reverent expectation the

close association of religious conformity and social life, and the class distinctions (particularly in England) created by or connected with the place of worship (church v. chapel) have been more harmful to religion than rationalist criticism, killing creativeness in religious art and literature.

71) *Pilgrims Progress,* edited by Edmund Venables, 2nd ed. Part. i, p. 140-41.
72) op. cit. p. 144
73) op. cit. p. 145
74) op. cit. p. 147-148. The above passage may be usefully compared with *Sir Owayn* and *Tundalus* (post, p. 88, 71)
75) Christian accounts of the death of martyrs, saints, virgins and children often mention the appearance of angels who bear the souls to heaven, and to visions of angels who bear the souls to heaven, and to visions of Our Lady or of some Patron Saint vouchsafed to virtuous people on their deathbed. Although this is very commonly found also in Mediaeval paintings and frescoes and votive pictures, such apparitions never assume the importance acquired by the Amidist *raigo,* a subject which deserves individual treatment. (v. pl.v) Mrs E.A. Gordon in her interesting study on the Lotus Gospel compared with Early Christianity (*World—Healers*), Tokyo, Maruzen, vol. 1 p. 203 ff.) refers to a wonderful 'mystery—procession' held annually at the Taemadera on May 14th, commemorating the reception into Paradise of the Princess Chûjô-himé who wrought in tapestry the famous Kwangyô mandâra, (753-781 A.D.) and became a nun in that monastery

(*Cathemerinon* V. De Novo Lumine Paschalis Sabbati. *Migne, Patr. Lat.* LIX, col. 826-7)

65) Florence, Palazzo Riccardi. v. pl. iv.
66) A profound difference exists between the Christian ascetic ideal of the Middle Ages with its condemnation of the body, and the Puritans' attiude. The latter seemed to have enjoyed dwelling upon the sins of the flesh, particularly all forms of sexual indulgence, and were often so busy ferreting them out and denouncing them that they had little time for thinking of the spirit. Hypocrisy, pruriency and false modesty which characterize the attitude of several centuries in England and across the Atlantic, made of the body a tyrant instead of the servant of man, thus defeating the very ends which such austerity was supposed to further. It is instructive in this respect to compare all this with the Buddhist meditations on the impurities of the body e.g. in the *Visuddhi Magga* cch. 1, 6.
67) quoted in Baillie, op. cit. p. 202
68) quoted in E. Steinilber-Oberlin, *The Buddhist Sects of Japan* (Eng. trs. p. 237)
69) The above applies also to those Catholic works in which lack of inspiration is hidden under virtuosity and where the artist represents the formal aspects of such states without any understanding of their spiritual significance.
70) cf. Baillie, op. cit. ch. 1, p. 4 ff. The question is thorny and controversial, nor is the phenomenon predominantly Protestant. Excluding individual cases however, the

55) ibid., 76-79
56) ibid., 95-114, 124-31
57) *Paradiso,* XXXI, 1-27
58) loc. cit..XXXIII, 55-57: 61-63; 82-90; 97-99; 115-20
59) ibid., 142-45
60) *Pearl,* edited by Sir Israel Gollancz, (Chatto and Windus, p. 248)
61) Milton, in *Paradise Lost* admirably expresses the Renaissance feeling that the loss of Paradise was, in the end, a gain for, through it man achieved a deeper and wider wisdom and knowledge.
62) A reference to the Trinity, i.e. the Father, the Son (the Lamb) and the Holy Ghost (flame of fire).
63) q.v. text and trs. of *Olympia* appended to Gollancz's ed. of *Pearl* cited above, lines 190-95; 200-224; 250-61; 263-71; 275-79.
64) cp. *Purgatorio,* XXVIII, 1-18; 28-42 quoted later, *Pearl,* ed. cit. stz. vii ff. and the following passage from Prudentius:

> Illic purpureis tecta rosariis / omnis fragrat humus calthaque pigria et molles violas, et tenues crocos / fundit uda fugacibus. /Illic et gracili balsamo surculo / deaudata fluunt, raroque cinnama / spirant, et folium, fonte quo abdito / praelambans fluvius portat in exitum. / Felices animae prata per herbida / concentu parili suave sonantibus / hymnorum modulis dulce canunt melos, / calcant et pedibus lilia candidis.

in that part of his *Confessions* (Bk. IX ch. x) where giving an account of the conference he had with his mother about the Kingdom of Heaven, shortly before her death, he describes it as a state beyond the soul "a region of never-wasting plenty, whence thou feedest Israel for ever with the food of truth, and where life is that wisdom by which all these things are made, both which have been, and which are to come."

49) It should be noted that this does not imply, however, a passive reliance upon the mercy of God, as is the case with the Amidists, but an active making oneself worthy of His mercy and grace. Heaven is not (like Nirvana) a supra-intellectual, intuitional abstraction. The Amidst conception of blessedness appears (at least in Japan) to arise as a reaction against such an idea, where emotion takes the place of the intellect and reason. Contradictory though it may seem, Amida is further removed from Christ than Sakyamuni is from Jesus as a comparison between the Amdist and the Christian Paradise shows.

50) *Paradiso*, XXVII, 109-114. The passages quoted are taken from Philip Wicksteed's prose version in the Temple Classics.

51) loc. cit. lines 4-9.

52) The exact nature of the bodily appearance assumed by the blessed in heaven and in the otherworld has been a source of great controversy. cp. the explanation given to George of Hungary by the Archangel Michael.

53) *Paradiso*, XXX, 64-51

54) ibid., 61-69

Mahomet, to which class, I would add, the vision of Andreas Salus mentioned on p. 46 does also conceivably belong. These apocalypses, closely related as they are to certain sacramental rites and mysteries, which embody the eschatology of the *Phaedrus* Myth, together with the influences of the Aristotelian *Metaphysics* and the *de Coelo* on the one hand, and the *Somnium Scipionis* and its antecedents on the other, are the lines along which, according to Stewart, the Platonic myth was transmitted to the *Paradiso* which 'reveals its parentage in nothing so clearly as in the character of being for its author, and even for ourselves, a *musterium*—a solemn ritual at which one may assist, not merely an admirable piece of literary workmanship.' (p. 368) The above remarks seem to confirm and illustrate admirably the essential 'functional' divergence between the Buddhist and the Christian paradise, referred to in the course of this essay.

45) It is interesting to compare this with the opening of the lotus in the Paradise of Amida. q.v. *Muryôjukyô* S.B.E. vol. xlix, pp. 192-99.

(S.B.E. vol. xlix, pp. 192-99.) Stewart, op. cit. p. 151, ff. draws attention to the remarkable parallell between Dante's account of those two streams and those found in the Orphic ritual from which Plato draws in the myth of Er (*Republic* 621)

46) Purgatorio, XI. 1-18, 28-42 (Shelley's trs.)

47) St. Bernard, Epist. ad Trasl. de Matre Dei, Lib. ii, (Migne, *Patrologia Latina,* CLXXXIV, col. 353-54.)

48) This has been admirably expressed by St. Augustine

nique shown in the poem and the radical change in taste, style and manner of representing the heavenly scene.

43) This does not apply to saints or saintly men, e.g. St. Paul and Andreas Salus.

44) v. post, p. 66 ff. A carefully detailed comparison between the Paradise and the Brahma heavens would be of considerable interest and throw some valuable light upon certain important parallels existing between the two conceptions of heaven from an astronomical and ethical point of view. Stewart *Myths of Plato,* p. 350 ff.) discussing Plato's eschatological myths, points out that in the *Phaedo* it is already made clear 'that the ultimate destination of the virtuous soul is not any Terrestrial Paradise, but a Celestial Paradise to which Pure Intelligence rises by its own strenuous effort.'; and that just as there and in earlier myths we have 'plodding feet and an *Inferno* and a *Purgatorio*', in the *Phaedrus* we have 'light wings and a *Paradiso*'. The eschatology of Dante, like that of the Pythagorean Orphics, is 'celestial and astronomical'. The *Paradiso* with its 'Ascension of a Purified Soul through the Moving Heavens into the Presence of God in the Unmoved Heaven' is, in effect, 'the latest embodiment of the Type (of myth) first made known to us in the Poem of Parmenides and the *Phaedrus* Myth'. The last canticle of the *Divina Commedia* was deliberately 'modelled not on the apocalypse of St. John, but on such astronomical ones as the *Secrets of Enoch* (cp. Appendix I (b) post.) the *Ascension of Isaiah* and the *Vision of*

tion of Our Lady.

39) Even more remarkable perhaps is the place occupied by her is art in which (in Catholic countries) she appears in her earthly and heavenly form as second in importance only to Christ. (cp. pl. ii)

40) In foreign works on Mahayana as well as in Japanese ones, the analogy is frequently drawn between the rôle of Our Lady and that of Kwannon. Such very superficial resemblances as may exist are very deceptive and do not bear close study. The Blessed Virgin always remains the earthly mother of Jesus-Christ (God) born in the usual manner. Even as Queen of of Heaven, the most perfect of saints but in no sense a divinity, she is neither the co-equal of God (as in theory is Kwannon) nor, as again in the case of Kwannon, an emanation of Him, but His creation like the rest of humanity. The functions of Kwannon, whether in the original or the later feminine form do not correspond to those of the Virgin except in so far as, being the Mother *par excellence,* she has and naturally come to be regarded as the special protector and symbol of perfect motherhood.

41) from J. L. Weston, *The Chief Middle English Poets,* p. 341: 11. 1-3, 24-28, 33-36, 41-42, 45-46, 51-54 73-80.

42) 'A. Hymn to the 'Name and Honor of the Admirable Sainte Teresa', lines 113-30, 133-144. It is hardly necessary to observe that the poem was in part suggested by Bernini's famous statue of the saint in ecstasy. Of greater interest is the tremendous advance in tech-

pp. 34-42) while referring to Byzantine painting, might well be applied, in a large measure, to the former:—

> There is no mistaking the divine nature of the Byzantine Christ—he is ever 'supersubstantial', and the Virgin is ever the Mother of God. Byzantine images of Christ and his mother differ from those of Mediaeval Western Art....One may not seek in them the humanity of the God-Man. The The sufferer is not in Byzantine art, nor does the Madonna weep for a crucified Son....Its stately mosaic compositions are magnificently decorative, harmonising with the forms and functions of the architecture they adorn, admirably seated. Their grace is not that of Nature's lithe pliancy, but the gracious stateliness of forms that move without movement, rythmic elements of great Church decoration. Beautiful colours are combined in balanced schemes showing a genius for colour values which may have come from the East....The drawing and colouring of the figures is religiously appropriate and decoratively beautiful. The majesty of Christ is unimpeached, the gracious dignity of God's Mother unexcelled. Angelic forms are not debased by any striving after naturalism in the representation of what is not of the earth. Their wings are of surpassing beauty, not made to fly with, but drawn to symbolize the celerity with which the Angelic nature does the will of God. (see pl. ii).

37) Roger Fry, *Vision and Design* (Phoenix Library, p. 146, Giotto)

38) v. *Legenda Aurea* by Jacopo da Voragine trs. by Caxton Temple Classics vol. iv, p. 234-71), sub The Assump-

29) ibid., vii, 9, 16-17`
30) ibid., xiv, 1-3
31) The precious stones mentioned are (in order): jasper, sapphire, chalcedony, emerald, sardonyx, chrysolite, beryl, topaz, jacinth and amethyst, each of which possesses a symbolic meaning according to the lore of precious stones. It is interesting to compare the list with that found in the *Smaller Sukhâvatî Vyûha* (Jap. *Amidakyô*) *Muryôjukyô* and *Amitâyur-Dhyâna Sutra* (*Kwangyô*) and with that of the *Mahâsudassana Sutta* (S.B.E. vol. xi). The latter which forms part of the Mahâvagga section of the *Dîgha Nikâya*, recalls somewhat the description of the Heavenly Jerusalem rather than that of the Christian paradise.
32) *Rev.*, xxi, 2, 11-13, 16, 18-19, 21-23.
33) ibid., xxii, 1-3, 5, cp. also examples from the *Apocalypse of Baruch* and *Apocalypse of Ezra* quoted by Charles in his *Critical History of a Future life* ch. vii.
34) *Anglo-Saxon Poetry,* selected and translated by R. K. Gordon. (Everyman's Library, pp. 154, 180, 181)
35) op. cit. p. 277
36) This may be clearly seen when comparing the treatment of the subject by Byzantine and later Italian painters, the former recalling the arrangement of the traditional frescoed *mandaras* and paintings of Amida's and other paradises found in the grottoes of Tung Huang, the latter Japanese works of the same nature but of a considerably later period, e.g. those of Eshin Sôzu (Genshin) 942-1017 etc. The following passage by Taylor (*The Classical Heritage in the Middle Ages*

universe is destroyed and renewed three times in each complete cycle (*mahâkalpa*), by water, fire and wind respectively, and with it all below the 10th Brahma heaven. The first period in each renewal is, in effect a kind of golden age. (q. v. Beal, *Catena of Buddhist Scriptures from the Chinese* p. 109 ff.). A similar conception is found in the Mazdean texts (e.g. the Avestic paradise of Yima). The myth of the destruction and renewal of the world is developed at greater length by later writers and assumes a deep religious and moral significance (q.v. Söderblom, op. cit. ch. 3. 4) as for instance in the *Politicus* (268E-274E). In modern times, it has been used for philosophical purpose by Leopardi in 'Storia del Genere Umano' which serves as introduction to the *Operette Morali,* to show how 'illusions' arise and perish.

24) v. *Preliminary Notes* quoted above, p. 31 ff.
25) v. Genshin's *Ojô Yôshû,* trs. by Reichshauer, Proc. A. S. Soc. Japan, 2nd. ser. vol. vii, sect. 6, p. 57 ff.
26) q. v. *Larger Sukhâvatî—Vyûha* (Jap. *Muryôjukyô*) trs. by Max Muller. Sacred Books of the East, vol. xlix, sect. 8-9, which contains Amida's vows.
27) In Protestant countries, especially England, the direct influence still persists. It may further be noted that in many cases, the popular conception of heaven at least, was partly moulded in the later Middle Ages and Early Renaissance, by secular works (drama and poetry) and that the latter came to have an influence often stronger than that of canonical ones.
28) *Rev.,* iv, 2-6

name is derived from Sukhadhara, the modern Socotra, an island off the East coast of Africa, well-known to Arab traders as one of the most beautiful and fertile spots of the earth, and also identified with the Island of Ka which was regarded by the ancient Egyptians as a kind of earthly paradise. (loc. cit. p. 95 ff.) Eliot (*Hinduism and Buddhism,* iii, p. 220 and n. y) observing that Sukuhâvatî differs from the abodes of bliss, and that it appears "suddenly in the history of B. as something exotic, grafted adroitly on the parent trunk, but sometimes overgrowing it", suggests the possibility of a connection between S. and the land of Saukavastan, governed by an immortal and located by the Bundeish between Turkistan and Chinistan, which seems to have been well known as a home of the blessed. Chinese mythology contains descriptions of several such mysterious islands, such as the Island of Ocean, in the Eastern sea, with a fountain that flows from a jade rock the waters of which ensure a long life and is inhabited by genii; the Island of Patriarchs where the plant of immortality grows and which restores the dead to life and others mentioned in the *Book of the Ten Islands* belonging to the Hand and Wei dynasties. Among these may also be placed the primeval paradise of the Sumerians, known as Dilmun, and supposed to be situated on the island of Bahrein, off the western shore of the Persian Gulf.

22) v. Hastings, *Encyclopaedia of Religion and Ethics,* s. v. Abodes of the Blest and passim.

23) According to Brahmanic and Buddhist cosmogonies the

contributed elements to the picture.

18) e.g. Hesiod, *Works and Days,* 167; see also Appendix I (a), post.

20) q. v. *Book of Revelation,* ch. 21 *and Book of Enoch* (trs. & edtd. by R. H. Charles), sect. V, CII etc.

21) q. v. Doi, *The old Japanese Myths and Traditions* (trs. of the Japan Society of London, vol. xxxv, pp. 101, -28 and ff. A further analogue is the pilgimage to the fabled Western Paradise ordered by the Chinese emperor Shin Huang Ti and placed in charge of the Taoist magician Sen She who failed to reach it and reported on his return that he had come within sight of the Islands of Paradise but had been driven back by contrary winds. The emperor despatched a second expedition with the order to bring back some of the 'Waters of Life' but this one also was unsuccessfull. Subsequently, many Taoist sages are supposed to have also visited or attempted to visit this magic island, which has frequently inspired artists and painters. A Han mounment dated about 145 A.D. found in an ancient cemetery near Chia-hsiang-hsien (Shantung province) bears on the upper part, a bas-relief showing the reception of the Emperor Mu Wang at the court of Hsi Wang Mu (the Royal Mother of the West) supposed to be situated in this Western Paradise, which—is has been suggested—(J.S.M. Ward, *The Hung Society,* ii, p. 31 f.) has contributed to the development of the legend of the Western Paradise of Kwan-Yin situated beyond the Western seas which, conceivably, may be a Taoist adaptation of Sukhavati. According to some this

that of George of Hungary. The divergencies referred be attributed, I think, to the somewhat conflicting opinions concerning heaven and paradise found in the Jewish religion—as a result of the conceptions derived from various sources incorporated into it—and to the new ideas developed or introduced by Christianity. Lazarus, to give an example, is referred to (Luke, xvi, 23) as having died and gone to 'Abraham's bosom', i.e. to a place of rest where he had communion with the saints, and enjoyed the same felicity with Abraham, the friend of God (as found in the O. T.). The later Christian belief, however, was that Abraham and the other patriarchs had been awaiting the coming of Christ in the 'Limbo of the Fathers' in some part of Hades which, according to some, was situated in the 3rd Heaven, and seems to correspond to Paradise. In the Apocalypse, Paradise is said to be the final abode of the righteous, while the Talmud describes in detail the degress of happiness up to that of supreme contemplation—found in the Garden of Eden.

It should further be remembered that the Christian happy otherworld was compounded largely out of many Aryan myths which were gradually harmonised and developed along two parallell lines. Thus giving rise to the conceptions of Paradise and Heaven which at times are, in practice, scarcely distinguishable to the ordinary layman.

17) cp. below p. 17, the passage from the *Phoenix*.
18) *Genesis,* ii, 8 ff. It seems also probable that the *Song of Songs* (iv, 12-16) and Jerahmeelite and other traditions

q. v. also De Visser, *Ancient Buddhism in Japan,* vol. ii, ch. xvi, and elsewhere under the various sutra headings. It is hardly necessary to add that references to the copying of sutras are also found in the *Genji Monogatari*.

11) cp. De Visser, op. cit., vol. i, p. 325 etc.

12) C.A.F. Rhys Davids, *Indian Religion and Survival,* p. 96 ff.

13) Betty Heimann, *Indian and Western Philosophy,* a Study in contrasts. p. 60-61.

14) cp. Heiman, op. cit. for an illuminating and scholarly exposition of the meaning of nirvana. In Mahayana Bud., however, N. is not in itself ultimate salvation although a fruit of it. For the Buddhist salvation is a matter of choice. Not to tread the path that leads to it, especially when this has been rendered relatively, easy through the vow of Amida is insensate, but it is not in any sense a failure in one's duty. In Christ salvation is an obligation, Son of God and joint-heir with Christ, the very life man enjoys or abuses and all else, including his body—the temple of the Holy Ghost—having been given to him by his Eternal Father.

A further important contibution to the literature on this subject is Dr. Hakuju i's study on Nibbana contributed to vol. I (1939) of *Studies on Buddhism in Japan* issued by The International Buddhist Society of Tokyo, (p. 39-52).

15) cp. post p. 42 the description of nirvana, quoted from the *Milinda Pañha*.

16) cp. post p. 65 ff. the vision of Sir Owayn and

7) Anezaki, *History of Japanese Religion,* p. 292

8) Revue de Métaphysique et Morale (Paris), Juillet 1936, p. 456 ff.

9) cp. Frazer, *Belief in Immortality and Worship of the Dead,* vol. i, p. 468:—

> "It is impossible not to be struck by the strength and perhaps we may say the universality, of the natural belief in immortality among the savage races of mankind. With them a life after dealth is not a matter of speculation and conjecture, of hope and fear, it is a practical certainty which the individual as little dreams of doubting as he doubts the reality of his own conscious existence. He assumes it without enquiry, and acts upon it without hesitation, as if it were one of the best assertained truths within the limits of human experience."
> (Quoted by Baillie, op. cit. supra.)

10) How significant an act of devotion was the transcribing of the sutra may be seen from the following quotation:

> If there be any who receive and keep, read and recite, rightly remember, practise and copy this Law-Flower Sutra, know that such are attending on Sakyamuni Buddha; know that the Buddha is praising them, know that the hands of such are being caressed by the hands of Sakyamuni Buddha, know that such are covered by the robe of Sakyamuni Buddha.... (*Lotus of the Wonderful Law,* trs. W.F. Soothill from the Chinese version, ch. xxviii, p. 263)

future life of the notions of human law and social justice existing upon earth. Whatever the differences between the various peoples in respect of the application of the law of retribution, the stress laid upon the idea or simple continuation (or immortality of the soul) which, in some cases, is regarded as a privilege not granted to all, suggests that in it may be found the germ of such future mythical imaginings as the garden of Eden, Paradise or ideal magic lands free from the disadvantages of life upon earth which, at a later period, are related to the idea of a separation among the dead in accordance with their merits or demerits upon earth.

3) q. v. n. 28 post. This is perhaps truer on the whole of the Old rather than of the New Testament. One is led to speculate whether the *Bible* would have come to occupy the position it still does in English-speaking countries, were it not for the Authorized Version. So far as I am aware the Buddhist *Tripitaka* in its various redactions is venerated for its contents which while recording, it is believed, the *ipsissima verba* of the Master, is not considered primarily even by non-believers as as a work of art. cp. pl. i.

4) John Baillie, *And the Life Everlasting*. p. 260-62

5) i.e. works of the Western School of painting, mainly in oils. A comparative study of the best examples of those in the traditional Japanese style, particularly if in black and white, is very illuminating. The difference, however, is less marked in the works of religious art inspired by Catholicism.

6) Anezaki, *Buddhist Art,* ch. IV

# NOTES

Preliminary Notes for a Comparative Study of Christian and Buddhist representations of the otherworld. *Annual Report of the Faculty of Literature,* Taihoku Imperial University (1937), pp. 1-45

The question will be discussed in a subsequent essay dealing with Hell and the purgatorial states. Söderblom in his comparative study *La Vie Future d'après le Mazdéisme* (Musée Guimet, Bibliothèque d'Etudes), illustrating the various beliefs in survival after death, draws attention to the important fact that where the destinies of the dead are found to be different: either a), their life upon earth differed (e.g. in Vedic times and among the early Egyptians) or b), their manner of death was different (e.g. Scandinavians, Esquimaux, Chinese), determining a difference in the fate of the dead in the afterlife. (p. 32 ff.) Later, the conception of the afterlife as a continuation of that upon earth and lacking any religious significance, undergoes a gradual transformation as the idea of retribution gains ground. The otherworld thus, in some cases, becomes a continuous retribution (though without a judge), or the departed are there punished for the sins or evil actions committed in it without any reference to those may have been guilty of while alive. (p. 47) The passage from the former to the latter conception is determined, according to Rohde (*Psyche*) by the transference to the

(as the great craftsmen, artists and writers of the Ages of Faith realized perhaps subconsciously—and a poem or a painting not less than a cathedral are acts of worship and love in the truest sense—are the twin pillars upon which visionary literature and all art indeed ultimately rest. They raise the spirit above the contingencies of this life and 'comfort man's mortality with immortal grace', but their authority comes not from this but from the Otherworld.

Arundell del Re

upon me considerable limitations and even within the restricted field chosen I am all too aware of having done but scanty justice to a theme so vitally connected with Eastern and Western art and literature. All specifically aesthetic, historical or ethnological considerations apart, I venture to suggest that even such studies as the presents one may be of value because they do throw greater light upon the fundamentally religious and social nature as well as upon the purposiveness of all forms of expression, whatever personal significance they may have for the individual; and upon the common human aspiration from which they spring, which may be summed up as the almost universal belief in a happy otherworld. That eschatological ideas play an all-important part in the spiritual and temporal life of mankind, is clearly proved by all the evidence at our disposal, and further corroborated by the passages quoted. Although contemporary civilization seems to demand that we should turn our eyes earthwards, rather than heavenwards, the Life Everlasting, however conceived, is still naturally and logically the supreme goal of man; it alone seems to hold within itself the key to the heart of absolute reality longed for by all, and to the achievement of that peace, born of Wisdom, that passes all understanding.

In every illustration given—whether from the West, from India or from East Asia—there is an underlying dominant note, a remarkable feeling of human solidarity quite independent of the religions in question and in spite of any dogmatic or philosophical divergence. As Robert Bridges has beautifully expressed it in the lines quoted at the beginning of this paper, it is Wisdom, 'the essential Beauty of Holiness', that makes men lovers and worshippers. Love and Worship,

to find a means of saving his family, the boy tells how he started out for the Hill of Hope where he thought he would find that which he was seeking. Along the long and difficult road he encounters three wild beasts, (168) but at that moment Jizô (169) appears before him, sent to save him in his quest. With him he enters the gates of hell, crosses the river Sanzu (which corresponds closely to Dante's Acheron) with a monster recalling Charon, (170) witnesses the judgment of Emma-O who is not unlike Minos, and the various punishment of the sinners, and subsequently is guided through the various heavenly spheres. From the report I have been given of the work through the courtesy of a well-known scholar Dr. Zanoni Volpicelli, it would appear that, quite independently of some of the details (parallelism between the conception of the otherworld in the *Commedia* and in Buddhism is not hard to discover, but does by no means possess great significance as an evidence of possible common sources), the structure of the vision, which differs substantially from that of Buddhist works of a similar nature, presents remarkable points of contact which do not seem to be wholly fortuitous. (171)

In the foregoing pages I have attempted to show in what expressive forms the idea of heaven, paradise or, more gererally, ultimate beatitude have been cast in Buddhist and in Christian lands, by setting side by side passages describing the abodes of the blessed. In doing this there has been no intention to try to establish any relation of dependence between them; such a task would indeed have been beyond my power even if the requisite data for so doing were at present available. The vastness of the subject has necessarily imposed

to the Palace of King Emma, the ruler of hell. As soon as they have returned to Kinpôsan the Zen priest, pointing to the East, shows him the castle of Mantoku Hoshuten, also known as the pope of Japan. Having traversed a wood glittering with trees of seven colours, they reach the place. Here the god gives him instructions as to how the people of Japan may placate the anger of the god of Daijôten who has been responsible for all the ills that have befallen Japan, and who has caused the wicked gods to exterminate Buddhism in order that the people should fall into the hells and evil ways. Through his instigation—he adds—such great temples as the Hôryûji, the Tôdaiji and the Enryakuji were destroyed by fire. But the Bodhissatvas of Kinpôsan and Hachiman have tried to help the people who foolishly do not understand that they must build temples to Daijôten and other gods who are protectors of the world. He, Doken, must henceforth cease to recite sutras and devote himself instead to the establishment of a great shrine called Nippon Daijô Itokuten, where in October and April, and especially at New Year, the Emperor and the people should pay homage to ask for the peace of the world and to placate the wicked gods and so bring back tranquillity. Having revealed all this he tells him to go back to his cave and to restore himself to life. Doken does as he is bidden by Hoshuten and returns once more to this world after a sojourn of thirteen days in heaven and hell.

Of quite a different type is the vision which Zennojô had while he lay in a faint in the snow. The remarkable analogies which it presents with that of Dante lead one to ask whether some knowledge of the Divina Commedia may not have reached Japan, through indirect channels, at that time Wishing

was governed and wished to drown those islands with all the tears they had caused him to shed during his lifetime, and to restore it after eightyfour years when all the heretics had been annihilated. Instead of this he had sent many bad gods to harm the country, but he, Doken, should be faithful to him and build temples and respect him as the first of all gods. If he will do this he shall have a long life, but if he does not he will only live 81 months,—instead of 81 years—as the paper given him says. The Zen priest and Doken then return to Kinpôsan. Then the priest leads Doken to the Tosotsuten (Tusita) heaven which lies to the south-west surrounded by a hedge of silver trees glittering with the seven treasures. Having passed through the treasure wood they arrive at a place the beauties of which cannot be described in words. In the wood there are many springs of clear water and gleaming crystal pools. The air is filled with melodious songs and music and d bodhissatvas are dancing and singing. As they wander through this paradise they meet with the Crown Prince of Japan, an Admiral and many famous Japanese priests, all of whom had been faithful Buddhists during their liftetime. At last they come into the presence of the god himself but they cannot see him because of the dazzling light that surrounds him. From a high throne Doken hears a noble and soft voice asking him why he has come here while he is still alive. To which the traveller answers: "I have come here through the supernatural powers of the Bodhissatva". Then the voice tells him that if he will continue to pursue the path of virtue he will come to this heaven after his death. On hearing this Doken is filled with joy and he and his guide return once more to Kinpôsan.

The next part of the work is concerned with Doken's visit

he remained for a period of six years. On hearing of the death of his mother re returned to that city and there spent some time not neglecting however to pay a visit to his monastery once a year. The country was then afflicted by many calamities and Doken, feeling that the only way to serve Japan was to practise religious austerities, abandoned the city again and for many years lived a hermit's life in a cave where he was joined by a young novice who desired to be instructed in the Law of the Buddha. One day, while he was building an altar, he was attacked by a very severe sore throat and fever and seems to have gone into a trance. As his spirit was seeking a path up the mountain side, a Zen monk with a golden vase filled with water and 28 children with lotuses in their hands appeared before him, carrying food and drink which they offered him for he was exhausted by his long fast and the pain. Taking him by the hand the monk leads him up the mountain, where golden light played among the trees, the trunks and branches of which were of gold with flowers of silver and bore golden fruit. Finally they reach a castle where the good Dwaijô sits enthroned who tells him that this is the paradise of Kinpôsan and that he is now a bodhissatva, and gives him a card on which are written the characters NICHI-ZOO. At that moment in the east shining with light, appears the God of the Daijôten heaven. As Doken expresses the desire to visit that heaven, the Zen monk leads him there on horseback. Soon they arrive at a vast lake in the midst of which is a large island full of sweet-scented flowers on which stands the shining palace of the seven treasures. The god Daijôten, who is the only inhabitant of this paradise, tells Doken that he was once a minister in Japan and that he was indignant at the way in which the country

Heaven as the ultimate goal and the beginning of immortal life beyond the grave granted to mankind through the merits of Jesus Christ, was and is shared equally by all Christians without distinction of sect. The same can hardly be said to be true of all Buddhists, thereby making of the happy otherworld a matter of individual belief rather than of absolute dogma, and thus altering—to a certain extent, the religious significance of such pictures.

Whether or not what has just been said has a definite connection with the character of the accounts given of the Otherworld and in particular of Paradise or Heaven, it is a noticeable fact that the otherworld 'vision' or 'journey' type of composition is very poorly represented in Buddhist literature. So far as I have been able to discover, there are only few examples of the latter kind of work properly comparable to those which have been illustrated above: the *Nimi Jataka,* (164) the *Gyôkureki* (165) (containing the description of the Holy Nichizoo's (Doken) visits to the heavens and the hells, and the *Kôkwan-Meishoroku* (166) known also as *Kantokuden*) describing the vision of a peasant boy named Zennojô. The first describes the journey of the virtuous Prince Nimi (one of Gautama's previous incarnations) to the pleaces of hell and heaven under the guidance of Matali the celestial charioteer where the situation, torments and pleasures of which are given dramatically and in detail. The second is of greater interest since the portagonist was a historical person and reference is made in it to numerous prominent personages of the time. At the age of 12 the young Doken entered the monastery of Kinpôsan (Kinbusan, not far from Kyôto) (167) where

popular character, Chinese as well as Japanese, often illustrated by rude wood-engravings and possessing little intrinsic interest or merit. Unlike what is the case in the West, the conception of the otherworld does not seem to have stimulated any organic work either in poetry or prose dealing with the subject, comparable to the Divina Commedia or to the poems of lesser writers quoted. (162) On the other hand it should be noted that this does not hold good in the field of art, which possesses such remarkable works as the famous Kitano Tenjin *makimono* in Kyoto—that may be truly described as having an epicodramatic character—and other scrolls, which are predominantly concerned with the representation, in a very lively and realistic manner, of the unhappy states, hungry ghosts, hell, and in a lesser degree of men, animals and *ashuras*. *Mandaras* of the various paradises seem to illustrate (at least in the earlier periods) the sutra descriptions, rather than to be original conceptions inspired by them, and only in the Kamakura period, under the influence of the Pure Land Sects does one find the otherworld represented as a unity, as may be seen from the few examples given by way of illustration. Apart from the practical considerations which determined the nature of such pictorial works (e.g. size and arrangement of the temples which unlike the Christian churches, did no as a rule so readily lend themselves to their permanent exhibition in a dominant position), it would seem that the purpose they subserved and the part they played in the religious cult was not analogous to that of similar Christian paintings or frescoes, (163) except in the case perhaps, of the grotto-temples of Central Asia and at the Horyuji. It might further be suggested that, however conceived, the belief in

from *Paradise Lost,* which serves to show how in Milton the Puritan spirit was tempered and coloured in great measure, by the Catholic tradition:

> ....................lowly reverent
> Towards either throne they (the Angels) bow, and to the ground
> With solemn adoration down they cast
> Thir crowns inwove with Amarant and Gold,
> Immortal Amarant, a Flower which once
> In Paradise, fast by the Tree of Life
> Began to bloom, but soon for man's offence
> To Heav'n remov'd where first it grew, there grows,
> And flours aloft shading the Fount of Life,
> And where the river of Bliss through midst of Heaven
> Rowls o'er Elisian Flowers her Amber stream;
> With these that never fade the Spirits Elect
> Bind thir resplendent locks inwreath'd with beams,
> Now in loose Garlands thick thrown off, the bright
> Pavement that like a Sea of Jasper shon
> Impurpl'd with Celestial Roses smil'd.
> Then Crown'd again thir golden Harps they took,
> Harps over tun'd, that glittering by thir side
> Like Quivers hung, and with Preamble sweet
> Of charming symphonie they introduce
> This sacred Song, and waken raptures high;
> No voice exempt, no voice but well could joine
> Melodious part, such concord is in Heav'n. (161)

Turning now to the Far East. The quotations already given in the preceding pages will have been sufficient to allow readers to form some idea of the Buddhist conception of Heaven and of the Pure Lands. In addition to the more or less canonical works there are also many devotional tracts of a

…nance for his sins—Tundalus, no less than George had been …ilty of much evil-doing—in order that he may be sure of …timately winning to heaven. As Tundalus obediently turns …vay from the contemplation of all this bliss, the soul suddenly …rows heavy and feels itself burdened with the body, and he …ice more opens his eyes to the mortal world.

To complete this partial picture of the Christian Paradise, … shall quote some lines on the lawns of Paradise as they are …escribed in that famous ancient Irish text.—The *Saltair na* …*ann* composed in the Xth century by three monks in the …orth of Ireland in which the traditional Celtic and the Christian ideas are blended together:

> The lawns of heaven, they say, are as wide as from here to the sun;
> Twelve of them, silver-soiled, and kind to the feet that run.
> All day you might travel that sward, nor be tired as we are here,
> For Paradise air is of ether; lustrous it is and clear:
> There's no wind to cast the blossoms in that place the sages call
> The Heaven of the Wondrous Ether;—no wind, nor breezes at all.
>
> But it's fresh,—the air—for the whole of it moves like the tide on the seas.
>
> Ample to nourish the flowering lands, the fruited trees.
> Each lawn has its silver rampart, its gate as wide as a mile,
>
>   And a bird, red-gold, above each gate, singing the while. (160)

Finally, by way of contrast, I add the well-known passage

> There was such sounds and such ringnig,
> Such melody and such singing,
> And such a sight of riches:
> There was more joy than any might guess. (157)

As Tundalus looks on amazed wishing that he might remain there for evermore, the Angel leads him to a great and lofty tree laden with all manner of fruit and flowers of many kinds and colours, in which were perched birds of divers hues singing melodiously and beneath it, dressed in rich garments, men and women who had endowed houses of religion and founded churches and chantries and helped the clergy. (158) And now they come to another wall made of precious stones set in gold, and climbing on to the top of it, Tundalus is told to look around him, and see what 'eye has not seen, nor eye heard, nor has it enterd into the heart of man, that which God hath prepared for them that love Him'. From there he may gaze upon the glorious company of heaven and see at one time all the joys and pains they had seen before and all the wide world and all the creatures created by God, as if in one single ray of the sun. Thus by virtue of the divine vision granted to those who stand on that wall, past and present, things far and near may all be comprehended in one glance without turning the head. No sooner does the desire to know something arise in the mind of Tundalus that it is immediately and fully satisfied because, as the writer explains, nothing can dim the sight of one to whom the sight of heaven has been once greated. (159) As in the case of Owayn and George, Tundalus begs to be allowed not to return again to earth, but the angel tells him that only those who have given their lives to the service of God may dwell here, and that he should henceforth make

another wall made of pure gold and within it a place with many thrones of gold upon which holy men and women were seated in robes of silk, their faces shining as the sun, and on their bright golden hair crowns of gold inlaid with many jewels 'of great virtue and various colours' so that they looked as if they were all kings and emperors. In front of each of them were golden lecterns on which lay books written in letters of gold. These are the souls of the martyrs who while still in the flesh tasted the joys of heaven. The writer then proceeds to give a detailed description of the many pavilions covered with purple and fine cloth and adorned with gold and silver, from the silken cords of which hang every kind of instrument of music which give out a delectable sound. Within men and women as bright as angels are singing sweetly and playing although he can see no mouth move nor do they touch any instrument with their hands. So great is the ecstasy induced by the sounds and perfumes wafted from them, that Tundalus forgets all the the other joys that he has previously experienced. Approaching closer he sees that from the shining ceiling numberless chains of fine gold are hanging, some richly enamelled, others festooned with the purest silver, and attached to them

> ....rich jewels and of great beauty,
> Vials and cups of great price,
> Cymbals of silver and fleur-de-lys,
> With silver bells, that merry rung;
> And angels flew them among
> With wings of gold, shining bright:
> No earthly man has seen such a sight,
> As the angels flew in the air,
> Among the chains, that were so fair.

tion and development of the Paradise theme barely outlined in Sir Owayn, but also because of the parallel it affords to the pictorial representations of Paradise by the great Italian painters of this period. It is furthremore interesting to set these beside the vision of Tundalus, with which they have some remarkable affinities, as well as significant differences.

In Tundalus the approach to Paradise is not across a bridge, but skirts a high wall within which a number of men and women with sad looks and suffering from hunger and thirst, are being tormented by wind and rain, but who are neither in darkness nor do they have to endure the stench of hell. These are they who after a period ofpunishment (purgatory) as a result of not having given to the poor and needy, will later enter paradise. The actual gate of paradise, of which no description is given, opens of itself and Tundalus and his angel-guide find themselves in a beautiful field full of scented flowers. Here there is no night nor does the sun set, and here too is a stream of living water which if anyone drink thereof he will thirst no more. This is the habitation of those who while not deserving punishment are not worthy as yet of entering into the full joy of the saints; here too is the golden house of King Cormac who having been unfaithful in wedlock suffers punishment by having to stand in flames up to the navel for three hours every day. (156) Proceeding further they now reach a wall made of silver, inside which Tundalus suddenly finds himself. Within are the souls of those who were faithful to their marriage vows, dressed in shining white robes and singing sweetly as they wander through the luminous scented air of the beautiful champaign filled with the songs of countless birds in the trees. And now they reach

regally adorned and on the other, somewhat lower, a most beautiful Queen, the sweetness of whose face and the beauty of whose figure could neither be painted nor described in words. Then prostrating himself before the Lord Jesus Christ and Mary the Queen of Heaven, George humbly asks Christ to bless him whereupon the Lord, lifting the cross in His left hand, blessed him and all the blessed, answered together 'Amen.' Then turning to Our Lady, he said the Angelic Salutation and the Blessed Virgin gave him her blessing and again all the heavenly host answered 'Amen'. (154) As George remains motionless, enraptured by the vision he has just seen, the Angel touches him and smiling asks him what he is thinking about and whether he would not like to remain there for ever. To which George replies that if such were the will of God he would never wish to return to earth, whereupon the angel explains why this may not be and that the saints alone live in heaven for evermore; this lower paradisiac region in which he now finds himself was, however, formed newly and created in the image and likeness of the Empyrean Heaven by God who, had ordered that the hosts of the angels and the blessed should descend there from their heavenly thrones and take on visible forms, that he, George, might while still subject to the laws of mortality and sin, accomplish the purpose of his pilgrimage and witness the glories of heaven in the likeness of a vision. And now, since all has been accomplished, the place where he now finds himself will completely vanish and the saints will immediately ascend again to heaven to abide with their Father and Lord, Jesus Christ. (155)

I have given a somewhat extensive summary of the Visions of George of Hungary, not only because they show the elabora-

of the living and the dead was lost by George. And now he
sees advancing from one side a multitude of angels in the likeness of young men, disposed in nine orders, singing 'Holy,
Holy, Holy .... Blessed is He that cometh in the name of
the Lord', and their song was so unutterably sweet that it
swept away every tribulation. It is followed by another great
multitude of men and women—patriarchs, prophets, doctors,
saints, martyrs, confessors and virgins also arranged in nine
orders—singing, and wearing golden crows or aureoles, and
dressed in robes according to their rank, some bearing golden
palms adorned with precious stones, or branches of trees also
of gold, or olive branches; others carrying all manner of musical instruments on which they played so that it seemed as if
the whole world were resounding with music and song. And
their faces and bodies shone brighter than the sun. Thus
George was able to look upon the glory of the Heavenly Host
with his earthly eye. Then Michael suddenly lifted George
up and placed him on the altar-shaped mound in order that he
should obtain a complete view of Paradise and of the blessed
who all enjoy the same beatitude although in different degrees,
according to their sanctity and charity. (153) As he was
feasting his eyes upon this wonderful spectacle, Michael said
to him, 'lift your eyes heavenwards and look upon the marvellous glories of heaven, and turning his eyes upwards, George
saw the heavens open and a great light pour forth that even
if innumerable worlds were set on fire could not be equalled
in intensity; and through the opening he saw a palace that
seemed to be burning with fire and was of indescribable beauty
and proportions, and in the midst of it two lofty glowing thrones, on the highest one of which sat the King

ave assumed such forms, nevertheless the place is not Paradise but an image and foretaste of its joys which God has been pleased to grant him. Proceeding further they reach a towering wall of gold shining brighter than the sun and in the midst of it a great closed gate which seemed to be of fire, and sent forth rays of light ten times keener than those of the sun, which did not burn but filled those who approached it with delight, joy and gladness such as no man could describe. And through the gate is wafted a perfume besides which all the perfumes of this world seemed as nothing. (151) This is the gate of Paradise, but not of the Celestial Paradise, beyond which George will see angels and the legions of the saints who look upon the face of God and have their seats in heaven and who, being spiritual substances until the resurrection day, are invisible to mortal eye. God, however, in his great mercy has ordered that they should descend from the Empyrean Heaven and assume the likeness of bodily shapes in order that he, George, notwithstanding his mortality prevented him from ascending into heaven, might nevertheless look upon its glories. Taking George by the hand, Michael leads him through the gate into a vast flat plain, extending foursquare, except for an elevation in the midst of it like unto an altar. Across this is an open space as far as the eye can reach, where neither flower, nor tree, nor herb nor any person or animal either large of small an be seen, and is paved with all manner of precious stones, forming a kind of picture in which the divers colours blend with one another. (152) So enrapturing is it to gaze upon, that one might never get tired of its beauty even after numberless centuries. Contemplating it hunger and thirst and every misery and all rememberance of this world and

waiting for him and he comes up through the hole amidst a beam of light, by which sign they knew

That he in Paradise had been,
And Purgatory's pains had seen,
And was a holy man. (147)

Reference has already been made to the number of pilgrims who penetrated into St. Patrick's Purgatory, and to the widespread popularity of the legend which came to be successively elaborated. Some interesting additional details as regards Paradise are found in the Latin account, in prose, known as the visions seen in St. Patrick's Purgatory by a Hungarian knight named George in 1353. (148) While in the Sir Owayn legend no mention is made of purgatory as a separate region, and it is only briefly referred to in the Vision of Tundalus, in the Visions of George, the idea is fully developed and the differences between purgatorial and infernal pains explained in detail. (149) After crossing the bridge, which has lost all its terrors, George and the Archangel Michael find themselves in an endless champaign, full of flowers of many colours which give forth scents of unutterable sweetness, completely flat and level like an altar, the delight of which was such that even if one were to continue walking across it for the space of a year it would seem as if one had not walked a mile. (150) Beyond this plain lies an exquisite pleasure-garden full of all manner of beautiful flowering trees, among the leaves and flowers of which divers birds are singing angelic songs, so that it seems to George as if he had been transported among choirs of angels and that this was indeed Paradise. But Michael tells him that while it is true that the birds are in truth angels who

rejoicing when they met like sisters and brothers. Some were dressed in scarlet or purple, others wore priestly robes and some cloth of gold, thus enabling the knight to identify their state and what they had been upon earth. While he is looking around him, the bishops join him again and after telling him about Paradise where they must rest for a long time before they can scale the height of glory—the Heavenly Paradise— where God sits enthroned, they lead him to a place where a mountain fair and high rises before them, from the top of which they can encompass the whole of the Earthly Paradise. Then they ask him to look upwards and to tell them the colour of heaven, whether grey or white, or blue or red or yellow or green. To which the knight replies that it was a thousand times brighter than the purest gold. That place, they continue, is only the entrance to Heaven, and every day through those gates sweet-smelling heavenly food is sent down to them to nourish their souls. And as they are speaking.

> A flame of fire, that sprang so bright,
> From Heaven's gate it fell,
> It seemed him there that, far and nigh,
> O'er Paradise that flame did fly
> And gave so sweet a smell; (146)

The flame alights on Owayn's head and by its virtue the power of earth is purged away. But now the time has come for him to return to earth by the same way he has come, and in spite of his earnest entreaties he has to leave them, and with a heart full of woe he retraces his steps, but this time the devils fly from before his face 'as bolts from a crossbow'. And when he finally reaches the sanctuary once more, he finds the monks

> There came two from the company
> And palms of gold they bare,
> And straightway to the knight they hied,
> And took him, one on either side,
> Archbishops both they were;
>
> And up and down they led that knight
> And many a joy they shewed to sight
> And mickle melody;
> . . . . . . . . . . . . . . . . . . .
> They danced in carols all a-row,
> Their joy, I trow, may no man know,
> Of God they spake and sung,
> And angels set the measure free
> With cithole, harp and psaltery,
> And bells that merry rung. (144)

Perched on the high trees he hears the birds of heaven rejoicing, lifting up their voices 'in many a changeful melody', and wishes he may abide there for ever. He also sees the Tree of Life.

> Gardens with flowers of diverse hue,
> The rose, the lily, there he knew
> Primrose and periwink;
> Mint, fetherfoy, and eglantine,
> 'Mid other flowers, and columbine,
> More than a man may think. (145)

Also herbs of all kinds such as are not found upon earth which remain eternally green and sweeter than liquorice; and wells of sweet water from one of which flow the four rivers which water the plain of Paradise. Some of the souls dwelled by themselves, others in groups, each one knowing the other and

(139) As Sir Owayn safely crosses the dizzy, razor-sharp bridge (140) to 'a better place', through the mercy of God and Mary,

> A cloth of gold to him was brought,
> But of its coming saw he naught,....
> That cloth he did on him that stound,
> And whole and healed the wounds he found
> Wrought by the fire's fierce flame. (141)

Looking beyond he sees a golden wall stretching as far as the eye could reach and a gate, fairer than any in this world 'all red gold and precious stone'—jaspers, coral, crystals, topazes, pearls, sapphires, rubies, onyxes, chrsopases, chalcedonies and diamonds—forming rich tabernacles with slender pillars and curved arches of carbuncles inlaid with bosses of red-gold, and surmounted by turrets of crystal. (142) These fair gates of Paradise open of themselves when Sir Owayn approaches and such a sweet perfume flows forth that

> The knight was of that sweetness fain,
> And drew such strength from it again....
> It seemed such strength to him were told
> He well might bear a thousand-fold
> More of such woe and pain;
> That he against the fiends to fight,
> Might well have turned him back forthright
> The road he came again. (143)

He now sees a procession advancing towards him with tapers and candlesticks of gold, preceded by a cross and gonfalon, and in it popes and cardinals, kings and queens,

separate secular from monastic life so far as the possibility of ultimate salvation is concerned, that followed upon the growth of the Franciscan and the Friar movement generally in Europe at the beginning of the XIIIth c., and almost two centuries earlier in Japan with the spread of the Jôdô and Shin sects. By reason of this, in practice as well as in theory, salvation is now to be found in the world as well as in the cloister; and plays a more intimately direct part in the shaping of everyday life, as paradise is brought within closer reach of toiling, suffering and sinning humanity.

In spite of the scepticism expressed by a few, the fame of the Sanctuary built on an islet in Lough Dergh over the entrance to St. Patrick's Purgatory and the otherworld (137), was fairly established by the XIIth century and lasted until the XVth, and soon came to occupy a unique position in Christendom as a place of pilgrimage even if only a few dared (or were allowed) to face the reputed terrors of the Purgatory itself. Of the accounts left of the experiences of such travellers, that of Sir Owyan Miles (138) is with reason held to be one of the most famous as well as the most interesting as regards the description given in it of Paradise. Unlike many other such accounts, it shows little dependence upon the *Phoenix* but includes several new features revealing the existence of the distinction between Paradise and Heaven previously mentioned. The stress laid by the unknown Middle—English author of the present recension on the poetical and imaginative elements of the story, gives his version a new freshness and a springlike feeling that recalls Chaucer's "Prologue to the Legend of Good Women", in vivid contrast with the didactic tone of the translation in the *Southern English Legendary*.

ed by Sir Owyan Miles, (129) and the *Vision of Tundalus.* (130) Both may be considered as examples of this kind of composition at its best (131), to which may be added, for purpose of reference and comparison, that of George of Hungary.

All belong to the class of visions already referred to, in which the writer is himself an actor. Such legends of pilgrimages or journeys to regions beyond the present world, either under the earth as in the stories of the heroes of classical and Norse mythology (132), or to some remote island (133) or distant land (134) for whatever purpose undertaken, are part of the vast body of what may be called 'the ocean of story', and embody universal themes treated in the heroic traditions of many peoples as well as in the later romances of chivalry. (135) Of all such enterprises, those to regions beyond the grave are the greatest and the most dangerous, but also those which afford the highest reward of all—the much desired knowledge concerning life after death and the future destiny of man. In the two legends previously mentioned, the visionary account of the otherworld is combined with the adventurous quest theme and treated dramatically. Their protagonists—and here perhaps the main significance of this further development lies—are  longer future saints or heroes, but ordinary men to whom, through the special grace of God, it has been vouchsafed to undergo such an experience and who are consecrated thenceforth to the task of imparting to others the saving wisdom thus acquired. (136) Whether the name be Owayn or Tundalus or Dante, in reality it is Everyman or, as Bunyan will later personify him, Christian. Such a secularization seems to reflect the general tendency to break down the barriers which

handling of the stories tends increasingly to vary as to detail, as the writers cease to be predominantly clerics and are concerned less with the dogmatic than with the dramatic and aesthetic posibilities of their material. The fact, moreover that they are writing in their native tongue for a public which is not interested in Latin and requires to be entertained as well as edified, makes their accounts of these imaginary or visionary pilgrimages to the otherworld, more personal and human: original compositions rather than translations. This, it may be added, is particularly noticeable in the descriptions of hell where the artist, possibly stimulated by the gruesome illustrated accounts of the tortures inflicted upon the early Christian martyrs, could give free rein to his imagination. As regards paradise, the position was somewhat different. It was obviously far more difficult to rise convincingly from the human to the spiritual and preternatural, than to descend to the subhuman and bestial. On the other hand, legends of a past golden age, of the lost paradise of Eden, the writings of the Fathers of the Church, and the natural human aspiration towards a region of perfect beauty, harmony and delight—an ideal background for chivalry and poetical romance—all contributed, in varying measure, to the creation of a beautiful imaginary picture, the authenticity of which the average believer would not be likely or indeed could wish to call into question.

Leaving aside such visions as those of Drichtelm, Furseus, Thurcill and writings of a similar nature in Latin, English, Italian, French, two works in particular are worthy of special notice both on account of their European fame and of their instrinsic artistic merits—*St. Patrick's Purgatory* as describ-

human terms of reference and possessed at the same time the essential requirements of a blessed land. The necessity for some distinction between the heaven of form and that of pure spirit—to use Buddhist phraseology—was clearly felt by Catholic writers and painters. The Protestant somewhat materialistic idea of a heavenly city (as already illustrated above) if not incompatible with the teachings of the Church, did not appeal aesthetically or logically to the Romance or Celtic temperaments. On the other hand the association of ideas between Paradise and a garden, quite apart from the etymological and semantic derivation of the word, may account for the natural tendency to fuse the Garden of Eden or Earthly Paradise and the celestial paradise—the difference being one of degree rather than of quality, and to create a distinction between paradise and heaven. (128) So much is evident from the mediaeval accounts of paradise given below. Such descriptions are, superficially, akin to the Early-English and other examples quoted and were certainly influenced by them, nevertheless they appear to fall into a separate category by reason of the stress laid upon the fact that Paradise is, in effect, an antechamber of heaven to which the souls of men will only be admitted at a later time, probably after the Last Judgment.

Vision literature, ecclesiastical and lay, occupies as is well-known, a conspicuous position among mediaeval writings by reason, somewhat unjustly, of its bulk rather than of its merits. With few exceptions, there is—as might be expected—little variety in the themes drawn from sacred and legendary Christian sources. The anonymous authors adhere fairly strictly to them in their descriptions of the otherworld, but the individual

a western mind immediately formulates as to the greater or lesser degree of spirituality in the respresentations of the Otherworld, has little meaning when applied to Buddhist art or literature, except in so far as it refers to the artist's ability to transcend the false notion of reality implicit in all form. The tropical luxuriance of detail which characterizes Buddhist art is less due to a desire to add—as in the West—new and more vivid embellishments, than to the working over of inherited motifs, themes, and symbols which serve to illustrate the traditional figure of the Buddhas and the Bodhissatvas or the beauties of the Western Land of Purity, get always as a materialized dream, not as a dreamlike reality, beyond human comprehension. (126)

As already observed, the conception of Paradise as a place a delights, a kind of pure land where all the deficiencies and impurities to which mankind is subject as a result of original sin no longer exist, and where the souls of the faithful departed may enjoy a foretaste of never-ending celestial bliss amid idyllic surroundings, not unlike those found in the Mahayana sutras, soon found its way into Christianity alongside of the conception of a supersensual heaven situated above the sky, the abode of the Holy Trinity, Our Lady, the Angels and the Church Triumphant. The early and far spread contacts between Christianity and many different people and races —Eastern and Western—who also possessed analogous traditions, as well as the story of the Garden of Eden attested by the Old Testament, all contributed to the progressive building up of a syncretic picture of paradise—half terrestrial, half celestial. (127) This region out of time while being beyond the actual material world, could be defined and described in

affected by the sufferings of any nor can they be injured. Thus they are able to visit freely the hot or cold hells in order to save their relatives. This is perhaps the most vital difference between the inhabitants of Amida's and those of the Christian paradise who are not allowed to visit Hell.

These passages from the description of Amida's Western Paradise afford many interesting points of similarity with the Christian one, more especially as portrayed in mediaeval poems and legends, and like the latter lent itself to pictorial treatment. (124) In this connection, it will be seen when comparing the representations of Amida's Paradise and those of Christian painters, that the latter often contain realistic touches not found in the former; while the earlier (mandara) compositions, approximate more closely to the early pictures of Heaven. In the later written descriptions, such details may be found, which would seem to indicate considerably greater freedom in the graphic arts Europe than in East Asia where traditional symbolism was preserved for a longer period. It might further be added that the desire for realism, or rather for bringing home more closely the conception of a paradisal state after death, is not so vital in Buddhism as it is in Christianity, since—it should be again stressed—the Western Paradise, much less Nirvana, do not exist objectively or in the world of sense. For the Buddhist all that we are accustomed to consider as real, is *ex hypothesi*, an illusion in which as it were, reality may clothe itself. In the view of some sects of the Mahayana, no formal distinction exists between this world and the next, except for those who are still blinded by error; and as the error is dispelled, the duality of I and Me gradually disappears. (125) The usual criticism which

wide radiance of sublimity so glorious that heart and words can not express it, and his eyes lose themselves in the path of clouds. (122)

The land of treasures is filled with the mysterious voices of the Law, and round him he sees golden palaces and bejewelled halls, and groves shining with great brilliancy and flocks of geese and wild ducks. The place is full of living beings from all parts of the universe, saints and others, some ascending into the sky, others among the forest trees, others again wading or bathing in the streams or singing and scattering flowers. Paradise is filled with a throng of beings who have a common life, see each other and hear each other's voice and seek after the same way. It is like 'a flourishing market-place.' There is no pain of parting, no bewilderment of passions, nothing which does not satisfy the heart. Possessing the gift of superior wisdom and that of 'mysterious communication', they can help their benefactors and understand what the heavenly beings, the birds, beasts and insects are thinking in their minds and what they are saying. If they wish to hear or to see any one in the universe they can do so without moving (123). Led by Kwannon and Seishi (Avalokitesvara and Mahasthama), the believers descend from their lotus seats and are brought to Amida and worship him. When they hear the 'way of soul sincerity, they enter into the sea of desire of universal wisdom. Tears of joy stream down like rain and a heart of deep desire penetrates to their very marrow.' Human beings and heavenly ones mingle, and all have a mind of mercy and mutually love each other 'with a love like that bestowed upon an only begotten son.' The marvellous diamond bodies of purity and strength are not

that they cannot be compared with what we have in the Human and Heavenly realms. The sweet and the sour are as the heart desires. Those who see the colour and smell the odour are made pure in heart. When they eat this good food their colour and strength are increased. When they have finished eating the tables disappear of themselves and then at proper time appear again. (116)

Of particular interest because a characteristic feature of most pictures of the Buddhist paradise, are the lotus lakes (117) and the pond of treasures adorned with the seven gems, strewn with golden sand, surrounded by gem trees, in which grow blue, yellow, white and red lotus-flowers 'in circumference as large as the wheel of a chariot'. Stairs made of gold, silver, beryl and crystal, one on each side, lead down to the lake. It is in these lakes that the newcomers to Amida's paradise are reborn within the calyx of a lotus, and it is on the lotus stand rising out of the treasure-pond that Amida is most frequently represented as sitting enthroned, flanked generally by Avalokitesvara and Mahasthama. (119) Around him various heavenly beings make all manner of music while 'their sleeves are blown by the breezes and they dance before him'. When a believer is born into this Paradise, according to the Ojo Yôshû, (120) he is like a blind man who has suddenly received the gift of sight. As he looks at his own body, his skin becomes radiant with golden rays, and he finds himself wearing gold rings, hair ornaments of beautiful feathers, a crown of gems, necklaces of wonderful jewels while his body is covered with undescribably beautiful ornaments. (121)

When he looks up into the spacious sky he beholds a

wonderful flowers, where all heavenly children live quite naturally, enjoying themselves in various ways, each with a garland of countless precious gems which shine 'just as if a hundred millions of suns and moons were united together'. (114)

Amida's land of bliss is rich in rivers of different kinds, some large some small but all delightful, which carry water of different sweet odours and bear branches of flowers. The sound of their waters is 'deep, unknown, incomprehensible, clear pleasant to the ear, touching the heart, beloved, sweet, delightful, never tiring, never disagreeable, as if it always said: "Non-eternal, peaceful, unreal". (115) On each side of these rivers are scented trees which overhang them; on them float lotuses and water-lilies, and there are also small islands inhabited by flocks of birds, and everywhere the air resounds with the voices of peacocks and sparrows, parrots and ducks, swans, cranes, and countless other birds. The waters utter whatever sound a man may wish to hear and fill him with the highest delight. But there is no sound of pain there, nor even the sound of 'perceiving what is neither pain nor pleasure'. It is indeed the land of heart's desire, where every wish is fulfilled no sooner than it has been formulated by its happy inhabitants, whether it be for raiment or ornaments, or palaces, or food, although the food tastes different from that of this world as Eshin Sôzu is careful to explain.

> If any, whether they be Bodhissatvas of the Pure Land, Rakan or any of the various beings, desire to eat, tables made of the Seven Treasures appear of themselves. These are laden with hundreds of kinds of delicious food and drink served in vessels made of the Seven Treasures.... The taste, the colour and the fragrance are so unusual

sometimes of one gem only, sometimes of two or more, disposed in seven rows, each of which is eight hundred *yoyanas* high All flowers and leaves have colours like the colours of various jewels, which emit beautiful rays. In addition to these seven rows of gem trees, the country is surrounded by groves of banana trees and by seven rows of palm trees (111) made of the seven gems and by seven terraces and by a golden net strung with bells. Lotus flowers made of all kinds of gems cover the country.

> Each jewel has rays of five hundred colours which look like flowers or like the moon and stars. Lodged high up in the open sky these rays form a tower of rays, whose storys and galleries are ten millions in number and built of a hundred jewels. (112)

In these galleries which are found in each division of the Buddha country, innumerable Devas play heavenly music.

> There are some musical instruments that are hung up in the open sky, like the jewelled banners of heaven; they emit musical sounds without being struck, which while resounding variously, all propound the rememberance of Buddha, of the Law and of the Church. (113)

As the gentle breezes blow through the intermingling branches of the trees, which are perfumed with heavenly scents, the ground is carpeted with flowers and their fragrance is wafted away, and enrapturing sounds proceed from the palm trees and the strings of bells moved by the wind, as 'from a heavenly musical instrument consisting of a thousand *kotis* of sounds, when played by Aryas'. Each forest tree is covered with seven sets of nets and between each are 500 million palaces built of

After making his broad eye lustrous, after driving away the darkness from all men, after removing all untimely misfortunes, he led hither those who dwell in Svarga (heaven) and who shine with endless light.

The splendour of sun and moon does not shine in heaven, nor the fiery splendour of the maze of jewels of the gods; the Lord overcomes all splendour, he, the bright one, who has performed his former discipline.

He is the best of men, the treasure of all who suffer; there is no one like him in all quarters. (107)

That world is prosperous, rich, good to live in, fertile, lovely and filled with many gods and men. But there is no essential difference between its inhabiants 'except when they are spoken of in ordinary and imperfect parlance as gods and men'. On every side the country is level, lovely like the palm of the hand, with districts full of jewels and treasures of every kind; nor black mountains, nor jewel ones. No mention is ever made there of fire, sun, moon, planets, constellations, stars or blinding darkness, or even of day or night except in the conversation of the Tathâgta, nor is there any idea of predial property belonging to monasteries. (108) In that world there are neither hells, nor brute creation, nor the realm of departed spirits, nor demons. (109)

Sukhâvatî is fragrant with many sweet scents, rich in manifold flowers and fruits, adorned with gem trees and peopled by tribes of sweet-voiced birds (110) made on purpose by Amida to proclaim the Law. These gem trees—one of the outstanding features of Sukhâvatî, are described in detail in the *Larger Sukhâvatî-Vyûha* and the *Meditation* Sutra. They are made of silver, gold, beryl, crystal, coral, red-pearl and diamond,

land is a wonderful paradise, in the etymological sense of the Persian term (garden), and that attention is paid only indirectly to architectural details, the principal stress being laid on its natural features. (104) At the same time in later times, it is reiterated that the Paradise of Amida (or of other Buddhas) is his magic creation, an expedient to save humanity, without an objective existence in itself, any more than the various 'transformation bodies' assumed at will by Buddhas and Bodissatvas. In this respect and bearing in mind the singular properties enjoyed by the inhabitants of these paradises, one is led to suggest that these were derived from or added to the most significant features already found in the various Brahmanic and Hinayanist heavens, in particular as regards the characteristics of those of the 5th Devaloka (Nirmânarati: Jap. Keraku) and of the Dhyana heavens—which had been duly modified to harmonize with the Mahayanist conceptions.

Sukhâvatî, the Land of Bliss, or as it is perhaps more popularly known in the Ear East, the Paradise of Amida, which gradually subsititutes that of Maitrya, contains within itself the excellences and good qualities of all the Buddha lands. (105) This dream-like country is situated countless millions of miles to the West and there 'a Tathâgata, called Amitayus, an Arhat, fully enlightened, dwells now, and remains, and supports himself, and teaches the Law.' (106) He,

> The lord of vast light (Amitâbha, incomparable and infinite) has illumined all the Buddha countries in all the quarters, he has quieted passions, all sins and errors, he has quieted the fire in the walk of hell.

which, together with the 4 Brahma heavens constitute the realm of form, clearly show that an attempt had been made to 'graduate' perfection by placing it in relation to the idea of purity, light and power. (101) Later, Burnouf when comparing the two systems, remarked that the Brahmanic conception predominates up to the Brahma heavens but that subsequently this is replaced largely by the Buddhist one which introduces new divinities and by the theory that the heavens and their inhabitants gain in might and purity in proportion to their elevation above the terrestrial world. (102)

In Mahayana Buddhism the heavenly regions seem, indeed, to lose much of their significance following the spread of the Pure Land ideas. Even in earlier times the heavens were mainly considered as the abode of the *devas* and gods, rather than as ultimate places of solace to which mankind in general might, through a virtuous life, hope to aspire, and never as a substitute for *nirvana*. While no doubts were raised as to the pleasures to be enjoyed in such realms, rebirth into one of them, if one took a long view of life and its ills, was viewed as an evil inasmuch as it delayed the final achievement of Bodhi. The 'pure land' on the other hand, quite apart from the important fact that it was within the reach of everyone (at least in theory), was felt to be, by its very nature, an important stage in the individual's spiritual career. Not only did it draw him out of the stream of rebirth but it placed him in exceptionally favourable conditions for hearing and learning the Law. The descriptions given of these paradises, whatever external influences may have in course of time contributed to their moulding, ultimately derive from those of the celestial regions (103), with this important difference that the whole

with worms and smell, and consuming fire and torturing worms, where 'those who defile themselves by working impurity' are punished. Then he was brought back to his room in the palace and 'by his side were the beautous forms of the maiden and of her companions, which stank more than filth and every kind of offal. And he began to think of himself.... and he was afraid and trembled at the idea of those tortures, which terrified him as he lay upon the bed....'(96)

The oriental origin of the excerpt becomes apparent even after a cursory reading both on account of its atmosphere as on that of such specific references to carpets, cushions, couches which seem to echo the descriptions of Prince Siddartha's apartments and the gardens and pools of the famous Palace of Righteousness found in the *Maha-Sudassana Sutta.* (97) It is further interesting to observe that while the Apocalypse of Peter mentions the existence of the sun, the non-existence of any visible or physical source of illumination is stressed—as here —in St. Andreas and in the *Phoenix* and is an essential characteristic of all paradises whether Christian or Mahayanist. (98) Not a less important feature shared by both paradises, is the absence of any inequalities in the beautiful landscape, which is flat and abounds in trees and watercourses, as will be seen from the texts quoted or summarized below. Before proceding however, it may be well to bear in mind that while the Buddhists appear to have taken over their cosmogony from the Brahmans, in so far as the general structure of the universe is concerned, they somewhat modified the essence of the underlying conception, to bring it into closer harmony with the fundamental moral teachings of Sakyamuni. (99) Rémusat was one of the first to observe (100) that the 14 heavens

enough. And he saw thrones ornamented with gold, and they were inlaid with precious stones and mother-of-pearl, and their splendour shone like the lightning, and the beauties thereof were of divers kinds. And there were there with the thrones couches which were furnished with cushions and carpets the splendour of the appearance of which overcame the splendour of the thrones; and the gladness inspired by their magnificence was beyond praise, And waters clear as crystal flowed forth, and they caused the beholder to rejoice with great joy.... And having taken the king's son round through the country the beauty whereof was so marvellous.... the men brought him into a city the praise whereof cannot be uttered. The fabric thereof was of fine gold, and the walls thereof were of stones the like of which no man hath ever seen. And who is able to describe the beauty of the city? Above it there flashed like lightning a light of twofold strength, which filled all spaces of the city. And there were soldiers there who were appointed each to his special duty, and to every rank of them was given a light which flashed like lightning, and by it they marched singing a sweet melody, which hath never been heard upon the tongue of man. And the king's son heard a voice which said, "This is the place of the perpetual rest of the righteous, and this is the joy of the gladness of those who have pleased God." (95)

As in the case of Sir Owayn, Tundalus and George, Prince Yewasef begged the men to give him a corner in the city where he might abide, but they told him that he could not yet live there, but would have to make himself worthy of it 'through much weariness and profuse sweat of the face, and thou must rule thy soul and make thyself to labour.' Then they took him to visit the abode of sinners—'places of darkness' filled

directly, may even have been responsible for what has been considered by some as a veiled allusion to Buddha in the *Paradiso*:

> 'A man is born upon the bank of Indus and there is none to tell of Christ, nor none to read, nor none to write;
> And all his volitions and his deeds are good so far as human reason seeth, sinless in life or in discourse. (93)

On the other hand Dante and his contemporaries were well acquainted with the 'spiritual romance' of *Barlaam and Jesoshaphat* (94). Even if they did not associate Marco Polo's 'Sagamoni Borcan, the best of men, a great saint in fact, according to their fashion', who 'an he had but been (a Christian) would have been a great saint of Our Lord Jesus Christ, so good and pure was the life he led' with St. Jesoshaphat — by its means they were brought into contact with the spiritual life of India, and with a somewhat different picture of paradise, as may be seen from the following passages:

> ....And he saw a vision wherein certain men, whose faces were most terrifying, snatched him up and carried him into places which he had never seen. And they brought him into a vast country wherein were many rivers, and the landscape thereof was very beautiful, and the perfumes of its flowers were exceedingly sweet. And he saw there trees of divers kinds growing all together, and they bore strange and marvellous fruits which were pleasant and most delicious to the taste. And the leaves of these trees sang sweet songs, and when they were set in motion there went forth from them delicious breezes of the sweetness of which the people could never have

other kinds, of birds all wondrously beautiful. Some shone like gold, others were white as snow, and all sang and warbled so sweetly that in truth Andreas could not say whether they were birds or angels, (90) for their chants seemed to reach up and pentrate to the highest heaven, and overcome by ecstacy, he loses consciousness.

But when he penetrates further into the forest he is greeted by even greater wonders which, nevertheless, if compared with the beauties of the regions of the blessed, would seem like horrible darkness. Having crossed a river (90), while wandering over a limitless plain where the trees moved by the breeze filled the air with an exquisite perfume and with celestial music he is transported suddenly, above the firmament supporting the sky, and finds beside him a youth whose face shone like the sun. I am unable to say with any degree of certainty to what extent this vision was generally known. Its interest however lies in the eastern luxuriance of the descriptions (92), some idea of which this pedestrian summary may have conveyed, and in such details as the music of the wind among the trees to which I shall refer again in connection with some of the descriptions of Buddha's Western Paradise. While it is not possible, at the present moment, to trace any definite dependence of the latter upon Christian or near-Eastern sources, it is worth indicating possible points of contact as they arise, which may eventually lead to the discovery of further cultural and artistic links between East and West in Central Asia.

Whether or not Marco Polo knew anything about The 'Pure Land', it is a fact that he was one of the first laymen to bring back to Europe an account of the Buddhist religion and, in-

ground; nor are there any rough slopes there at all. But the noble field is fruitful under the sky, blossoming in beauty. (86) That radiant land is twelve fathoms higher (so wise sages in their wisdom tell us from hearsay) than any of the mountains, which here with us rise aloft in brightness under the stars.... (87) Winter and summer alike the forest is hung with fruits.... The groves are hung with blossomings, with fair fruits; there the ornaments of the forest, holy under heaven, never fade; nor do the yellow fruits, the beauty of the trees, fall to the ground there.... There is no foe in the land, nor weeping, nor woe, nor sign of grief, nor old age, nor sorrow, nor cruel death, nor loss of life, nor the coming of a hateful thing, nor sin, nor strife, nor sad grief, nor the struggle of poverty, nor lack of wealth, nor sorrow, nor sleep, nor heavy illness.... (88)

Another, and somewhat later description of the paradisal regions and of the Empyrean is that given in Nicephorus' life of St. Andreas Salus (89) written about 950 A.D. Andreas, who lived in Constantinople was carried up through paradise to heaven in a trance to find himself, garbed in a shining snow-white tunic, adorned with jewels, his head crowned with a wreath of flowers, in a wonderful garden that shone with a mysterious light which poured forth from diverse-coloured flowers 'which imitated the rays of the sun'. The place abounded in trees of a very different nature from those found upon earth, for 'they bloomed for ever and emitted a delicious perfume while a honey-like liquor oozed from them', and their lofty crests interlocked. Their beauty was not unlike that of the firmament and the pleasure they engendered was too great for his senses to bear. Some bore fruit, others flowers, others leaves, all equally beautiful. In them were sparrows, cicadae and countless

.... Et le Seigneur me montra, dit-il, une région fort vaste, en dehors de ce monde, resplendissante de lumière, et l'air de ce lieu illuminé par les rayons du soleil, et la terre fleurie de fleurs qui ne fanent point, et remplie d'essences aromatiques et de plantes aux belles fleurs qui ne se flétrissent pas et portent des fruits bénis. Or, tel était le parfum de ces fleurs qu'il arrivait de là jusqu'à nous. Quant aux habitants de ce lieu, ils étaient revêtus du vêtement des anges radieux et leur vêtement était en harmonie avec leur séjour. Là, des anges circulaient autour d'euxs. La gloire des habitants de ce lieu était égale (pour tous) et d'une même voix ils saluaient avec allégresse le Seigneur Dieu en ce lieu.... (85)

The theme as set forth above gradually was elaborated by subsequent writers but, in the main, the details remain unchanged except for the reference to the existence of the actual sun. The *locus classicus* is the famous poem by Lactantius (IVth c.) *De Ave Phoenice,* part one of which describes the Earthly Paradise situated in the East 'afar off from evil-doers a land 'dowered with delights, with earth's sweetest scents'.

.... There often to the blessed the delight of harmonies, the door of heaven is set open and revealed. That is a fair field, green forests spread beneath the skies. There neither rain nor snow, nor the breath of frost, nor the blast of fire, nor the fall of hail, nor the dropping of rime, nor the heat of the sun, nor unbroken cold, nor warm weather, nor wintry shower shall do any hurt; but the land lies happy and unharmed. That noble land is abloom with flowers. No hills or mountains stand there steeply, nor do stone-cliffs rise aloft as here with us; nor are there valleys or dales, or hill-caves, mounds or rising

mighty and boundless like the Ocean and, like the Ocean, 'all in blossom, as it were, with innumerable and fine flowers of purity, of knowledge and of emancipation.' (82) And though 'there is no spot....either in the East, or the South, or in the West, or the North, either above, or below, or on the horizon....where Nirvana is—yet, concludes Nagasena—as the man who has eyes wherever he may be....on a mountain top or in the highest heavens—will be able to behold the expanse of heaven, and to see the horizon facing him just so, O king, will he who orders his conducts aright and is careful in attention,....attain to the realisation of Nirvana.' (83)

One of the works that exercised an even greater influence than the Apocalypse of St. John upon those later writers whether religious or secular who undertook to describe the regions beyond the grave, is the Apocalypse of St. Peter accepted for many years as a canonical work. The manuscript, discovered in the necropolis of Akmin in Upper Egypt in 1886-87, contains the concluding lines of a discourse made by Christ on the otherworld followed by his revelation to St. Peter of the tortures of the damned and the joys of the saved. As will be seen from the passage quoted, the place described is a kind of earthly paradise, not unlike that in *Olympia,* and possessing the traditional qualities associated with it—abundance of flowers, sweet scents, and trees that ever remain green. An important point is that the blessed are dressed like angels and that angels move amongst them, possibly a reminiscence of that mythical age when the 'sons of God came to the daughters of men', (84) and that the place is lit up by the rays of the sun, although as specifically stated, it was situated outside this world.

in that street, O king, these bazaars are open—a flower bazaar and an antidote bazaar, and a medicine bazaar, and an ambrosia bazaar, and a bazaar for precious stones, and a bazaar for all manner of merchandise.' (78)

After mentioning the various subjects of meditation prescribed by Buddha, symbolized by the flower bazaar, Nagasena goes on to speak of those who by practising them have been set free, and after crossing 'the ocean of Samsara' enter that 'glorious city, spotless and stainless, pure and white, ageless and deathless, where all is security and calm and bliss—the city of Nirvana.' (79)

Here, in the bazaars the Blessed One has opened for the salvation of man, one may acquire the perfume of righteousness and the fruits of happiness and peace, antidotes that deliver from the poison of evil dispositions, and the medicine of truth which frees man from old age and death, and that ambrosia by which gods and men 'are set free from rebirths, old age, disease and death, from grief, and lamentation, and pain, and sorrow, and despair.' Furthermore the Blessed One has adorned his children with certain jewels (80) and they 'shine forth in splendour, illuminating the whole world of gods and men, brightening it in its depths, in its heights, from horizon to horizon, with a brilliant glory.' The City of Righteousness is inhabited by Arhats and by those who have entered the way, by men endowed with right conduct or accomplished in meditation, by the wise and the contemplative, by joyful lovers of solitude and by the earnest and the prudent who feed on little and know no greed. (81) Of such is 'that most blessed city of Nirvana, peaceful and calm, where no fear dwells',

Jerusalem is afforded, I think, by the purely allegorical picture of Nirvana found in the *Milinda Panha,* quoted below. Unlike the Pure Land paradises or the Christian conception of a Paradise of Delights, Nirvana no less than Heaven is, by its very nature, outside of space and time and the life of the senses:— a state of perfect beatitude—which is none the less real and true for not being susceptible of definition. (76) Nagasena, unlike Bunyan and many others, does not set out to describe the imaginary city, (knowing well that no such city does or can exist) but uses the allegory of the City of Righteousness, as Bunyan does that of the Heavenly Jerusalem, to convey the meaning of Nirvana (or, in the latter case of Heaven) to King Milinda. (77)

'....that Blessed One, peerless, unequalled, unapproached, incomparable, admirable,....full of virtue and perfection, boundless in wisdom and glory and zeal and power, who, when he had attained to the summit of all the perfections of the Buddhas,....he, bursting asunder the net of heresy, and casting aside ignorance, and causing wisdom to arise, and bearing aloft the torch of Truth, reached forward to Buddhahood itself, and so, unconquered and unconquerable in fight, built this city of Righteousness. And the Blessed One's City of Righteousness O King, has righteousness for its rampart, and fear of sin for its moat, and knowledge for the battlement over its city gate, and zeal for the watch-tower above that, faith for the pillars at its base, and mindfulness for the watch-man at the gate, and wisdom for the terrace above, and the Suttantas for its market-place, and the Abidhamma for its cross-ways, and the Vinaya for its judgment-hall, and constant self-possession for its chief street. And

abode of God and His elect, such as it was presented to and took shape in the popular imagination. Its main source, the *Book of Revelation,* need not be insisted upon further, but it is worth drawing attention to certain features which have the purpose and the effect of bringing heaven closer to man. While—as might be expected—the human element is completely absent in *Revelation,* we can find it in the atmosphere of the Early-English passages quoted, rather than in any specific detail. This tendency becomes more marked in the Middle-English and later periods where as the illustrations will show, one cannot but feel that heavenly bliss is not a very remote vision, but a reality that lies within the grasp of the earnest believer. Above all, in the 'Orisoun' as in the *Pilgrim's Progress,* the Blessed Virgin, the Saints, and God himself, no less than the loved ones who have gone before, have a personal interest in the welfare and the salvation of the individual. Such conceptions were the natural development of the teachings of the Christian Church based upon scriptural authority and on such favourite parables as that of the Good Shepherd and the Prodigal Son, as well as of the cult of the Virgin and the Saints (in Catholic countries),— the latter presenting some remarkable analogies with the growth of the Bodhissatva doctrine in Northern Buddhism,— and of popular beliefs concerning the Guardian Angels. Another detail worthy of notice is the vivid illustration Bunyan gives of the assurance universally held that the souls of the departed will come to welcome all newcomers to the Heavenly Kingdom, which might be considered as finding an analogue, in some measure, in the Amidist *raigo.* (75)

An interesting parallel to the description of the Heavenly

When they approach the gate they are met by a company of the Heavenly Host and by several of the King's Trumpeters, dressed in '...shining raiment who saluted the pilgrims with loud and melodious noises which made the heavens echo', and escorted them to the gate over which was an inscription in letters of gold.

> Then I saw in my dream that the shining men bid them call at the gate; the which when they did, some from above looked over the gate, to wit, Enoch, Moses, and Elijah etc.... and then the pilgrims gave in unto them each man his certificate, which they had received in the beginning. Those therefore were carried in to the King who, when he had read them....commanded to open the gate....
> Now I saw in my dream, that these two men went in at the gate; and lo, as they entered, they were transfigured, and they had raiment put on that shone like gold. There was also that met them with harps and crowns and gave them to them.... Then I heard in my dream that all the bells in the city rang again for joy ....Now just as the gates were opened to let in the men, I looked in after them; and behold the city shone like the sun, and in it walked many men, with crowns on their heads, palms in their hands and golden harps to sing praises withal. There were also of them that had wings, and they answered one another without intermission, saying Holy, Holy, Holy, is the Lord. And after that, they shut up the gates: which when I had seen, I wished myself among them. (74)

The various passages which have been, perhaps arbitrarily, grouped together although belonging to different ages, will serve none the less to give a clearer picture of the

would enter it. When they have crossed it, they find the two shining men waiting for them on the other side who greet them saying:

> ....We are ministring spirits, sent forth to minister for those that shall be Heirs of Salvation. Thus they went along towards the gate. Now you must note that the City stood upon a mighty hill, but the Pilgrims went up the hill with ease, because they had these two men to lead them up by the arms; also they had left their mortal garments behind them in the River; for though they went in with them they came out without them. They therefore went up here with much agility and speed, though the foundation upon which the city was framed was higher than the clouds. (72)

There on Mount Sion, in the Heavenly Jerusalem, was the Paradise of God where they would see the Tree of Life and eat of its never-fading fruits, and be given white robes and walk and talk every day, for all eternity with the King.

> ....In that place you must wear crowns of gold, and enjoy the perpetual sight and visions of the Holy One, for there you shall see Him as He is. There also you shall serve him continually with praise with shouting and thanksgiving, whom you desired to serve in the world though with much difficulty, because of the infirmity of your flesh. There your eyes shall be delighted with seeing, and your ears with hearing the pleasant voice of the mighty One. There you shall enjoy your friends again, that are got thither before you; and there you shall meet with joy even every one that follows into the Holy Place after you. There also you shall be cloathed with glory and majesty, and put into an equipage fit to ride out with the King of Glory.... (73)

lies between the two work separated far less in time than they are in the nature of the faith on which they rest. This becomes clear if one compares the idea of heaven in the two—that of Dante, logically and spiritually acceptable today as it was in the XIVth century, that of Bunyan, unacceptable and deprived of meaning except as a beautiful allegory, while still remaining an invaluable document testifying to the vital evolution of eschatological ideas.

> Now I saw in my dream, that by this time the Pilgrims were got over the Inchanted Ground, and entering in the Country of Beulah, whose air was very sweet and pleasant ....Yea, here they heard continually the singing of birds, and saw every day the flowers appear on the earth, and heard the voice of the turtle in the land. In this country the sun shineth night and day....Here they were within sight of the City they were going to: also here met some of the inhabitants thereof; for in this land the shining ones commonly walked, because it was on the borders of heaven....Here they had no want of corn and wine; for in this place they met with abundance of what they had sought for in all their pilgrimage. (71)

From here they had a more perfect view of the city 'builded of pearls and precious stones', with streets paved with gold, 'so that by reason of the natural glory of the City, and the reflection of the sun-beams upon it, Christian, with desire fell sick, Hopeful also had a fit or two of the same disease.' Having recovered somewhat and being 'better able to bear their sickness' they go on their way and are met by two men in 'raiment that shone like gold, also their faces shone as the light', who show them the gate of the city which lay on the other side of a deep river, through which they must pass if they

more subtle quality, as Dante shows us. Such a demand made on the believer, whether spectator or artist, implied a living, reasonable faith, which the age of Reason without Faith that measured the heavens in terms of man, could not give. To this one might also add that the criticism expressed in many Protestant religious quarters of the 'traditional view' of heaven, and the modernistic demand for a new interpretation of it in more 'spiritual' terms, has arisen partly owing to the influence of the picture of it given by Bunyan and the Nonconformists and partly through the absence of true religious faith on the part of the teachers and exegesists. (70)

The picture I have tried to present however, would be incomplete without some illustrations from *Pilgrim's Progress.* Bunyan's vision may be said to have been to the Puritans what the Legend of St. Patrick's Purgatory and similar works were to the English Catholics of the Middle Ages. It carries on, in some measure the 'morality' tradition with its personalization of virtues and vices, weaving them into an epico-dramatic narrative written in homely prose. A martyr to his beliefs, Bunyan became a symbol of religious individualism and his work a simple but practical guide for those who, flying from the wrath to come, left the wilderness of the world in search of the Heavenly City. It is important to note that Bunyan, like Honen and Shinran, preached the way of salvation not by retiring from the world, but by living in it yet not being of it; thus serving as a living example to others. The whole work is—no less than the *Commedia*—an allegory of life's pilgrimage the prize and crown of which is the finding of the Holy City promised by Christ to all who believe in him and do his commandments. Yet what a profound abyss

take the place of depth of feeling. Apart from singing, processions, and pageantry and the greeting of newly arrived souls, life in the heavenly regions has become formalized and seems strangely lacking in true spiritual activity when compared with that of the earlier ages. From the fact that the artists of the Renaissance show a marked preference for representing less the glories of heaven as such than as a contrast to the terrors of hell on the day of the Last Judgment, one may also infer that the conception of blessedness which inspired earlier painters and writers had been lost, thus producing the effect of dullness already referred to. (69) Whatever the cause, heaven became largely meaningless, not because blessedness cannot be conceived or represented by humanity, as is so often repeated,—Dante's Paradise, the *Ojo Yôshû* and other works in the East and in the West clearly show this not to be the case—but through a failure to meditate upon its meaning and to understand the nature of the spiritual experience upon which it rests, of which the external representation is, at best, only a pale shadow. However vaguely, the mediaeval artists and writers might understand this, they conveyed to others the conviction that behind the more or less materialistic or allegorical language, which they felt to be sadly inadequate to describe the paradisal state, there was an intense spiritual activity, a reaching forward towards a wider, and fuller realization of a beauty and happiness essentially different in quality from that found upon this earth. In a sense the achievement of heaven was the beginning and not the end. The dramatic element in Paradise far from being absent is even stronger perhaps than in the nether regions, but it requires to be pitched much higher and to be of an infinitely

Spiritual' with its felicitous combination of naive religious fervour, semi-barbaric realism and natural melodies springing from the heart, which has a grandeur lacking in most of the hymns after the 16th century but is found in the great religious chants of the Mediaeval Church. It would be unfair to omit, however, that the realistic heaven of simple joys easily appreciated by all, the outstanding features of which are the triumph of righteousness and the **reward** of the chosen rather than of the virtuous, played a very important part in the religious and social life of a large section of Christianity on both sides of the Atlantic

A further point which may be noted in connection with Catholic and Protestant writers such as Bunyan and some of his predecessors, is that allegory no longer, as in earlier ages, is a means to an end, but becomes an end in itself, either justifying realism and excusing intellectual conceits, or merely as a useful instrument for preachers, having little or no connection with the deeper truths of spiritual revelation. In almost all the later representations of heaven indeed, the main appeal seems to be to utilitarian or sentimental feelings.

Evidences of a strong, deep, personal religious experience, become increasingly hard to find and are substituted by outward lipservice to or formal acceptance of ethical and religious principles, due less to inner conviction than to the pleasurable feeling of self-righteousness induced by doing unpleasant things, thus making religion a means of immolation of self and others on the altar of self. The pleasures and joys of heaven are of a despairing sameness and lack life or inner conviction. Even in the Hymn to Saint Theresa, fine though it is, emotional rapture and technical dexterity,

> Thy bulwarkes diamonds square,
> Thy gates are of right orient pearls,
> Exceding rich and rare....
>
> Thy gardens and thy gallant walkes
> Continually are greene.
> There groes such sweete and pleasant flowers
> As noe where else are seene....
>
> There cinomon, there sugar groes
> There narde and balme abound.
> What tongue can tell or heart conceive
> The joyes that there are found? (67)

The spirit of the hymn is remarkably close to that of one of the psalms composed by Shinran Shonin:—

> Seek refuge in the heavenly harmony.
> The alleys of Paradise are full of trees
> Laden with jewels and precious stones,
> Which quivering all together and with a same rhythm,
> Emit exquisite sounds and make delicious music.
>
> Seek refuge in the Divine Promise,
> In the Treasure of Merit!
> From the seven gem-laden trees
> Emanates a sweet-smelling perfume,
> The flowers, fruits, branches and leaves of Paradise
> Set aquivering their colours and lights. (68)

The Christian conceptions of heavenly bliss hitherto mentioned however, so far as aesthetic stimulus is concerned, can hardly be said to have been very active or creative in Protestant Europe. None the less they were the source of that very original form of 'spiritual' song known as 'Negro

In the passages quoted we have, in classical dress, a humanist picture of paradise largely similar and in detail if contrasting in spirit with that drawn by mediaeval writers and, particularly, by Dante, (64) and such as later was to find perfect artistic realization in Benozzo Gozzoli's fresco of Paradise in Florence, and in the work of later painters. (65)

The Renaissance and the Reformation, the one positively, the other negatively, through the curious inverted sensualism of the Puritans (66), pressed the claims of the individual as a microcosm and the all-importance of humanity, overstressing on the one hand the divinity of man *per se* forgetting his origin, and obscuring, on the other, the true nature of the heavenly vision. Not content with bringing the latter down to earth, they made it earth-bound in an attempt to attract the more educated without ceasing to appeal to the simple. In Bunyan this Puritan side of the process of 'de-divinization', if so one may call it, reaches perhaps the highest point of development. With the Book of Revelation, for starting point, it crystallised and helped to spread a picture of heaven which has since become traditional in the Non-conformist English sects and finds expression in many hymns which imitated, for the most part unsuccessfully, those of an earlier day such as the beautiful 16th century 'Hierusalem, my happy Home', adding thereto elements derived from other sources which recall the descriptions of the Earthly Paradise and the Promised Land, 'flowing with milk and honey'. The few verses quoted below will be sufficient to give a better idea of how heaven was pictured by the common folk and others, for many centuries—

Thy walls are made of precious stones,

Then comes the Snow-white Host (virgins); lilies their brows
enwreathe. To these joined our little band,
thy children fair. The Saffron Order next,
illustrious, resplendent, with loud voice
sing praises of the Gods, and serve the King...

Olympia then proceeds to describe the Virgin Mary:

Jove's gracious Mother She, daughter eke,
the Gods' Queen-Mother, Heaven's Gem, Night's Bane,
Celestial Star, the Shepherds' certain hope,
their flocks' sure guard, their wish'd-for rest from toil!
Fauns Her adore and nymphs; Apollo great
with lute exalts Her praise, and owns Her Queen.
She worshipful, upon the Father's throne,
on right-hand of the Son, full brightly shines.
Her looks the woods and mountains, hills and poles,
make glad. Too fair is She. About Her fly
white swan-like bands; as Mother hail they Her,
as Spouse and Daughter of Eternal Light!...
We youths cull flowers; and, with the wreaths we make,
our unshorn locks we crown. With dances glad
we circle woods and founts and sounding brooks;
and, sporting 'mid the grasses, with loud voice
we chant due praises of the gentle Maid;
and eke the Son we laud. The wood's delights
who can recount? Who tell in words? Not one!
First must he put on wings, as bird by flight
to seek and see the heights; else all is vain...
Thy brother feed, give to the weary milk,
to prisoners alms; the naked clothe, the fallen
raise, whilst thou canst; take strangers to thy home.
Such offices will give the eagle's wings;
and God thy guide, thou wilt to Heaven fly.— (63)

ever-green and 'peace-loving olive-trees dear to Pallas.' The place is full of sweet-scented flowers and soft zephyrs; silvery streams meander here and there with murmur sweet, and there are gold-hued' birds and 'gold-horned goats', and gentle deer, and lambs with snowy fleeces gleaming 'with brightest gold'; and oxen, bulls, cows all resplendent with gold; 'yea, lions tame, and griffins tame, their manes with gold all bright'. It is Elysium, a region of perpetual spring, untroubled by southern gales.

> a joyous calm the place pervades. Earth's mists,
> and Night, all things that jar, are banished thence.
> Death comes not to the flocks, nor ailing age;
> and far are grievous cares, and want and grief.
> Things wished for freely come to all....
> High, on a grassy mound, in glory sits
> Acesilas (God), sheperding flocks and worlds.
> But, verily, would'st thou His aspect know,
> it were in vain; the mind this cannot grasp.
> All life is He, too fair, wholly serene;
> and in His bosom rests a Lamb, milk-white, (Christ)
> sweet sustenance for folk, whereby we live;
> thence comes our weal, and life to those re-born.
> And from Them both alike there flames a fire, (62)
> wondrous to trow! To all things spreads that light:
> the sad it comforts, purges the mind's eye,
> counsels the wretched, strengthens those that fall,
> with sweetest love informs the souls of men.
> An aged band of Satyrs (saints), suppliant,
> their hoary locks with rosy chaplets crowned,
> stand there; with lute and song the Lamb they praise.
> And then the Purple Order (martyrs) well revered,
> their temples all engirt with laurel green.
> At cross-roads these with pipes the true God sang,....

Oh! but how scant the utterance, Dante exclaims, how impossible to express the mystery in logical terms, before the 'high fantasy' power fails him, but

> already my desire and will were rolled—even as a wheel that moveth equally—by the Love that moves the sun and the other stars. (59)

Before passing on to consider another group of representations of the heavenly regions, it may be of some interest to illustrate the effect upon them of the first revival of classicism as shown in passages from Boccaccio's XIVth Aeclogue (Olympia), written about 1361. The differences between this work, the *Pearl* and Dante's description of the Earthly Paradise in the *Purgatorio,* are all the more remarkable if one bears in mind that Boccaccio was not only a worshipper of the memory of Dante and a devoted student of his works but an early pioneer of the Renaissance, one who 'characteristically, under the influence of his great Italian Master, harmonized Virgilian form with Christian belief.' (60) The process of humanization which gradually continues throughout the Renaissance, ultimately leads to the secularization of Christian art but, unlike what occurs in Protestant countries, is less the result of the materialization of heaven than of the peopling of it by an idealized, semi-divine humanity, an apotheosis of Man almost in the Shelleyan sense. (61)

Olympia, (Boccaccio's daughter Violante who died as a child) appears to him in a vision and describes the heavenly kingdom (Olympus) where she now dwells among a 'god-like throng' on the summit of a mountain, bright with perpetual light, adorned with towering palms, with festal laurels, cedars

storm! (57)

But the crowning grace of Dante's whole pourney, the revelation of the final goal of Divine Providence and of the great mysteries of the Incarnation and the Redemption is finally granted him through the intercession of Mary and the saints. His sight has became pure and he is able to see more and more clearly into the **ray** of the deep light 'which in itself is true'.

> Thence forward was my vision mightier than our discourse, which faileth at such sight, and faileth memory at so great outrage....
> ....yet doth the sweetness that was born of it still drop within my heart.
> ................
> O grace abounding, wherein I presumed to fix my look on the eternal light so long that I consumed my sight thereon!
> Within its depths I saw ingathered, bound by love in one volume, the scattered leaves of all the universe;
> substance and accidents and their relations, as though together fused, after such fashion that what I tell of is one simple flame.
> Thus all suspended did my mind gaze fixed, immovable, intent, ever enkindled by its gazing.
> ................
> In the profound and shining being of the deep light appeared to me three circles, of three colours and one magnitude.
> One by the second as Iris by Iris seemed reflected, and the third seemed a fire breathed equally from one and from the other. (58)

me—as who doth hold his peace yet fain would speak—Beatrice drew, and said: "Behold how great the white-robed concourse so filled that but few folk are now awaited there... (56)

Then, the supreme vision of the Church triumphant and the Angels:

In form then, of a white rose displayed itself to me that sacred soldiery which in his blood Christ made his spouse;

but the other, which as it flieth seeth and doth sing his glory who enamoureth it, and the excellence which hath made it what it is,

like to a swarm of bees which doth one while plunge into the flowers and another while went back to where its tail is turned to sweetness,

ever descended into the great flower adorned with so many leaves, and reascended thence to where its love doth ceaseless make sojourn.

They had their faces all of living flame, and wings of gold, and the rest so white that never snow reacheth such limit.

When they descended into the flower, from rank to rank they proferred of the peace and of the ardour which they acquired as they fanned their sides,

nor did the interposing of so great a flying multitude, betwixt the flower and that which was above, impede the vision nor the splendour;

for the divine light so penetrateth through the universe, in measure of its worthiness, that nought hath power to oppose it.

This realm, secure and gladsome, thronged with ancient folk and new, had look and love all turned unto one mark.

O threefold light, which in a single star, glinting upon their sight doth so content them, look down upon our

Then as inebriated with the odours they plunged themselves again into the marvellous swirl, and as one entered issued forth another. (54)

But this is only a last symbolic mask for

...The river and the topaz-gems that enter and go forth, and the smiling of the grasses are the shadowy prefaces of their reality. (55)

And as Dante continues to gaze upon the scene, the flowers and the sparks change into 'ampler joyance' of the mystic rose,

....so that I saw both the two courts of heaven manifested.

O splendour of God whereby I saw the lofty triumph of the truthful realm, give me the power to tell how I beheld it.

A light there is up yonder which maketh the Creator visible unto the creature, who only in beholding him hath its own peace;

and it so outstretcheth circle-wise that its circumference would be too loose a girdle for the sun.

All its appearance is composed of rays reflected from the top of the First Moved, which draweth thence its life and potency.

And as a hill-side doth reflect itself in water at its foot, as if to look upon its own adornment when it is rich in grasses and in flowers,

so, mounting o'er the light, around, around, casting reflection in more than thousand ranks I saw all that of us hath won return up yonder....

Within the yellow of the eternal rose, which doth expand, rank upon rank, and reeketh perfume of praise unto the Sun that maketh spring for ever,

> Light and love grasp it in one circle, as doth it the others and this engirdment he only who doth gird it understandeth. (50)

To Dante drinking in its glory from the swiftest heaven, it seems as if he

> ....was beholding a smile of the universe; wherefore my intoxication entered by hearing and by sight.
> O joy! O gladness unspeakable! O life compact of love and peace! O wealth secure that hath no longing! (51)

When Dante and Beatrice reach the Empyrean heaven, where time and space exist no longer, the lights and the symbolic visions of the lower spheres are quenched, and for a moment he is surrounded by the pallour of emptiness and turns to Beatrice who now appears of such transcendent beauty 'that only he who made it enjoyeth it complete'. Then Beatrice tells him that they have now issued forth into the heaven of light, love, and joy which is beyond space, where he will behold the elect in the forms they will wear after the resurrection of the dead, at the end of the world. (52)

> As a sudden flash of lightning which so shattereth the visual spirits as to rob the eye of power to realize even the strongest objects;
> So there shone around me a living light, leaving me swathed in such a web of its glow that naught appeared to me.... (53)
> And I saw a light, in river form, glow tawny betwixt banks painted with marvellous spring.
> From out this river issued living sparks, and dropped on every side into the blossoms, like rubies set in gold.

to mind a great Romanesque cathedral, with its elaborate yet effective symbolism of man's ascent to God, through Christ, wherein the *Paradiso* not only symbolizes the great mystery of the Redemption, but may be likened to a solemn chant that swirls and rises to the vaulted roof mingling with the dancing motes of coloured light that pour through the stained glass windows, the dominant note of which is the outward expression of the mystery of the Divine Love embracing and containing all other loves, and defined by St. Bernard as 'the supreme essence from which all comes; the supreme substance not subject to verbal predicates, but subsisting as the causal principle of all things in which our being does not die, our intellect does not lose its way, our love is not offended: that is ever sought after, that we may find it sweeter, and is found to grow sweetest when we most diligently seek it. (47) More than life without death, or pain or sorrow or disease, more than a supra-sensual or an intellectual life of a new kind, Heaven is the fruition of God and, in the classic words of Boethius 'the complete possession of unlimited life all at once'; the ability to see all things sub *specie quaedam aeternitatis*. (48) This is not, however, in any sense, an intellectualistic conception as in Buddhism, or one to be achieved through the mind. It is a revelation granted to those who have actively given up their will to and identified it with that of God (49) whose will 'is our peace', and the fulfillment of which makes of the *Paradiso* a paradise indeed that

> ....hath no other *where* than the divine mind wherein is kindled the love which rolleth it and the power which it sheddeth.

> .... Water of purest hue
> on earth, would appear turbid and impure
> compared with this, whose unconcealing dew,
>
> Dark, dark, yet clear, moved under the obscure
> eternal shades, whose interwoven looms
> the rays of moon or sunlight ne'er endure.
>
> I moved not with feet, but mid the glooms
> pierced with my charmed eye, contemplating
> the mighty multitude of fresh May blooms
>
> Which starred that night,..when, even as a thing..
> that suddenly, for blank astonishment,
> charms every sense, and makes all thought take wing,—
>
> A solitary woman! and she went
> singing and gathering flower after flower,
> with which her way was painted and besprent (46)

As will be seen, while accepting the doctrine of the Earthly Paradise which symbolizes the perfect happiness of life in the flesh according to St. Thomas Aquinas and some theologians, Dante unlike other writers does not describe it in detail, thus avoiding the confusion often made between its temporary and somewhat materialistically conceived joys, and those of the celestial paradise, outside of space and time.

What is perhaps most striking in Dante's vision—one may hardly call it representation—of the glories of Paradise, is the use he makes of light, colour and sound images to convey the ineffable, where the symbols, however important, are accessories rather than an end in themselves. In this respect he might perhaps be called the first expressionist. If we look at the *Commedia* in its architectural entirety, it naturally brings

significance. It does not only afford a foretaste of the joys of heaven but, what is more important, it is here that Dante is brought to a full realization of the errors committed in the past and to repent; and having drunk of the waters of the river Lethe that wipe out the past, and of those of Eunoë which restore memory of the good within him and rekindle the light in his soul,—he is now made a new man, 'pure and ready to ascend to the stars'. (45) The picture he gives of

> the divine wood, whose thick green living woof
> tempered the young day to the sight...

is classical in its simplicity and serenity. With slow, soft steps he winds

> up the green slope, beneath the forest's roof,
> ....leaving the mountain's steep,
> and sought those inmost labyrinths, motion-proof
>
> against the air, that in the stillness deep
> and solemn, struck upon my forehead bare...
>
> In which the leaves tremblingly were
> all bent towards that part where earliest
> the sacred hill obscures the morning air.
>
> Yet were they not so shaken from the rest,
> but that the birds, perched on the utmost spray,
> incessantly renewing their blithe quest,
>
> With perfect joy received the early day,
> singing within the glancing leaves, whose sound
> kept a low burden to their roundelay,...

His advance is stopped by a small stream, the

Osborn Taylor phrased it—'literal fact, moral teaching, and allegorical or spiritual significance'; a *'Summa* of saving doctrine, which is driven home by illustrations of the sovereign good and abysmal evil coming to man under providence of God.' At the same time, it is the drama of his own enlightenment and progress towards ultimate salvation through perfect love which is perfect knowledge. Other wayfarers in the regions of the beyond had themselves suffered some of the punishments inflicted upon the wicked (Tundalus), but none of them except Dante had been actually lifted up into the heavens (43), or had attempted an organic and logical description of the three realms, distinguishing—as he has done—their subhuman (Hell), human (Purgatory), and superhuman (Paradise) characteristics, and making them live for his readers without doing violence to the intellect or the spirit. For these reasons Dante's vision is more than a work of 'licensed imagination', it is the exposition of a real spiritual and intellectual experience, neither a nightmare nor a dream. Not without reason does he claim 'the water which I take was never coursed before', when referring to his Paradise. Knowing well that 'to pass beyond humanity may not be told in words', he makes no attempt to describe, by physical imagery what is purely spiritual, and perhaps deliberately avoids the use of the traditional symbolism of the Apocalypse which if not imitated none the less colours the allegorical pageant of the Church in the Earthly Paradise, which in some respects recalls the descriptions found in Sir Owayn, in Tundalus, in that of Alberic of Montecassino and, more closely, in the *Visio Georgii*. (44)

In Dante the Earthly Paradise has a special purpose and

The Moon of maidens stars, thy white
Mistress, attended by such bright
Soules as thy shining self, shall come
And in her first rankes make thee room;
Where 'mongst her snowy family
Immortal welcomes wait for thee.
  O what delight, when reveal'd Life shall **stand**
And teach thy lips heav'n with his hand;...
What joyes shall seize thy soul, **when she**
Bending her blessed eyes on thee
(Those second Smiles of Heav'n) shall **dart**
Her mild rayes through thy melting heart!
  Angels, thy old friends, there shall greet thee
Glad at their own home now to meet thee.
  All thy good Workes which went before
And waited for thee, at the door,
Shall own thee there; and all in one
Weave a constellation
Of Crowns, with which the King thy spouse
Shall build up thy triumphant browes. (42)

\*    \*    \*    \*    \*

The vision of Dante differs essentially from all other visions of the otherworld. Like them it has its basis in the teachings of the Church and a religious purpose, nor is there any reason to believe that he did not accept such teachings as true. Unlike them, however, it is a poetical and theological presentation of the beliefs concerning the otherworld held by mediaeval Christianity which affected, in many different ways, the imagination of succeeding centuries. The *Commedia* springs from the life upon earth to enfold 'the three-fold quasi-other world of damned, of purging, and of finally purified, spirits.' It is a drama of action and suffering which offers—as Henry

> There they quaff, from cups of gold,
> Draughts of life, with bliss untold...
> White the robes thine household wear,
> Crown of gold doth each one bear;
> White as lily, red as rose,
> Glad the songs that each one knows!...
> Mercy aye is found in thee,
> None who trusts thee lost shall be.
> Save thy Son, all things above,
> In my heart I do thee love!
> Heaven fulfilled is with thy bliss,
> Earth with this, thy gentleness:
> Such thy grace, thy mercy free,
> None lack help who cry to thee!... (41)

By way of contrast, and as an example of the process of humanization referred to at its highest, and which has its parallel in the arts, I quote from Crashaw's magnificent 'metaphysical' Hymn to Saint Theresa. Its combination of mysticism and sensuousness, so different from the direct simplicity of the 'Orisoun', is of particular interest as illustrating how the later Renaissance tried to achieve a harmonious balance between the life of the spirit and that of the senses.

> Like a soft lump of incense, hasted
> By too hot a fire, and wasted
> Into perfuming clouds, so fast
> Shalt thou exhale to Heaven at last
> In a resolving Sigh, and then
> O what? Ask not the Tongues of men.
> Angels cannot tell, suffice,
> Thy self shall feel thine own full joyes
> And hold them fast ever. There
> So soon as you first appear,

*Legenda Aurea* (38), nor the writings and devotion to Our Lady of St. Jerome, St. Francis of Assisi, St Bernard and countless others, nor yet her miracles that served to enthrone her in heaven and in the hearts of men, so much as the fact that She was the mother of Christ and as such symbolized all the beauty, tenderness, self-sacrifice and suffering of motherhood, and a mother's understanding love—a perfect example of womanhood—and a willing intercessor for man. Thus she appears in the *Commedia,* in the Mediaeval visions, in art (39) and in the mystery plays. While in no way usurping, as some Protestant writers assert, the role of sole mediator belonging to Christ, she is associated with him in the minds of all Catholics, a perpetual reminder of the mystery of his divinity and humanity, a human link between Heaven and Earth. (40) This may clearly be seen in the following lines from the beautiful early 13th century 'A Good Orisoun of Our Lady'.—

> Christ's dear Mother, Mary mild,
> Light of life, Maid undefiled,
> Low I bow and bend the knee,...
> None in Heaven thy peer shall be;
> High thy throne o'er Cherubim,
> Christ thou see'st 'mid Seraphim;
> 'Fore thee angels merry sing,
> Music make with carolling,...
> Of thy friends thou makest Kings;
> Royal robes, and golden rings
> Thou dost give—and rest full fair,
> Safe from sorrow, death or care...
> There they rest who served thee here,
> Kept their lives from evil clear...

ever increasing tendency to work over the traditional material, to elaborate and embellish it with all the resources and skill at the artist's or writer's disposal; to make it on the one hand, more worthy of the great themes treated and, on the other, to render these more readily apprehensible to the lay folk and so inspire them to turn heart as well as eye heavenwards. The process of 'humanization' is already well advanced; and, with it, disappears the 'supersubstantiality' of the Byzantine heaven, while the heavenly regions acquire a new richness of lively expression. (36) Dante, like Giotto, was the greatest epic-painter as well as the greatest story-teller, reconciling actuality and universality. For the men of Giotto's day as for those of Dante's, what they represented by line or word must, in a sense, hold the mirror up to everyday life, or at least be such as might easily be converted into human terms. At the same time it 'was necessary that they should possess that quality of universal and eternal significance which distinguishes a myth from a mere historical event. It was even more necessary that they should be heroic than that they should be actual.' (37)

What Roger Fry says above has an important bearing upon the evolution of the conception of heaven and paradise, and is particularly true of the unique position which is held by the Blessed Virgin Mary and, later, by some of the saints and apostles. While no reference to her appears, for obvious reasons, in the Apocalypse, she is found, shortly after her death occupying—as Mother of God—a place in the Empyrean second only to that of Christ, and playing a very significant part in the Liturgy of the Church. But it was not only the beautiful description of her death and assumption in the

....O the fair heavenly trinity, filled with glories, high and holy, blessed far and wide throughout the spacious plains.... Wherefore they, diligent, crowned with glory, the righteous race of the seraphim, ever uttering praise on high with the angels, sing with unwearied strength very loud, with a great voice, sweetly far and near. They have the best of ministries with the King. Christ granted that their eyes may delight in his presence, brightly arrayed and with their wings they guard the presence of almighty God, the Lord eternal, and throng about the throne all eagerly striving which of them in the courts of peace may in his flight flutter nearest to our Saviour....

There shall be the song of angels, the delight of the blessed; there shall be the dear face of the Lord brighter than the sun for all the happy ones; there shall be the love of friends.... a glad multitude of men the glory of the blessed; day without darkness, radiant, full of spendour....there is the joy of angels, peace and happiness, and rest for souls; and there for ever and ever they who perform his behests here on earth may make merry and rejoice with the Lord. He holds for them in heaven a reward everlasting, where the highest King of all kings rules the city. Those are the buildings which decay not.... (34)

A radiant crown wondrously fashioned of precious stones shall rise over the head of each of the blessed. The heads shall gleam, gloriously covered; a princely diadem shall adorn with rare beauty each of the righteous brightly....where, girt round with glory, they shall dwell in beauty amid fair adornments, with the Father of angels. (35)

The quotations just given are a good example of what might be called the gradual change in the spiritual climate of the age as regards the idea of heaven, shared with minor differences, by the whole of Christianity, and derived from common sources. In the arts as in literature, there is an

voice of great thunder: and I heard the voice of harpers harping with their harps: and they sang as it were a new song..... (30)

And I John saw the holy city, new Jerusalem, coming down from God out of heaven, prepared as a bride adorned for her husband.... having the glory of God: and her light was like unto a stone most precious, even like a jasper stone, clear as crystal, and had a great wall and high, and had twelve gates, and at the gates twelve angels.... On the East three gates; on the north three gates; on the south three gates; and on the west three gates.... And the city lieth foursquare.... And the building of the wall thereof was of jasper: and the city was pure gold, like unto clear crystal.... And the foundations of the wall of the city were garnished with all manner of precious stones.... (31) And the twelve gates were twelve pearls; every several gate was of one pearl: and the street of the city was pure gold, as it were transparent glass. And I saw no temple therein: for the Lord God Almighty and the Lamb are the temple of it. And the city had no need of the sun, neither of the moon, to shine in it: for the glory of God did lighten it, and the Lamb is the light thereof. (32) And he shewed me a pure river of water of life, clear as crystal, proceeding out of the throne of God and of the Lamb. In the midst of the street of it, and on either side of the river, was there the tree of life, which bare twelve manner of fruits, and yielded her fruit every month, and the leaves of the tree were for the healing of the nations. And there shall be no more curse.... and his servants shall serve him: and they shall see his face.... And there shall be no night there; and they need no candle, neither light of the sun: for the Lord God giveth them light: and they shall reign for ever and ever. (33)

To illustrate further the treatment of the theme and the development of certain of its motives, I give a few passages out of two famous Early English works—'Christ' and 'The Phoenix', both of which belong to the 8th century.

tions of the day of judgment in addition to certain passages from the prophetic books of the Old Testament as well as from the New. In this respect its influence on the popular imagination and on the arts either directly, or indirectly through sermons and other homiletic writings, cannot easily be overestimated. Much of its symbolism, through the Authorized Version of the Bible has become a part of the English linguistic inheritance. (27) Although familiar to many, I quote below a number of passages that may serve t ogive a fairly adequate idea of the main lines of St. John's conception.

...... and, behold, a throne was set in heaven, and one sat on the throne. And he that sat was to look upon like a jasper and a sardine stone: and there was a rainbow about the throne in sight like unto an emerald. And round about the throne were four and twenty seats: and upon the seats I saw four and twenty elders sitting, clothed in white raiment; and they had on their heads crowns of gold. And out of the throne proceeded lightnings and thunderings and voices.... And before the throne there was a sea of glass like unto crystal... (28)

After this I beheld, and lo a great multitude, which no man could number, of all nations and kindreds, and people and tongues, stood before the throne, and before the Lamb, clothed with white robes, and palms in their hands....They shall hunger no more, neither thirst any more; neither shall the sun light on them, nor any heat. For the Lamb which is in the midst of the throne shall feed them, and shall lead them unto living fountains of waters: and God shall wipe away all tears from their eyes. (29)

And I looked, and lo a Lamb stood on the mount Sion, and with him an hundred and forty and four thousand, having the Father's name written on their foreheads. And I heard a voice from heaven, as the voice of many waters, and as the

joy presided over by Aksobhya (Ashuku), in the East, and the Paradises of Maitreya, Sakyamuni and numberless others of lesser importance and beauty—represented as the materialization of a state having no objective existence (all empyrical reality being *ex hypothesi* transcendentally unreal): a kind of magic vision, having all the appearances of reality, created by Amida or other Buddhas for the salvation of mankind. (26)

Eschatological studies generally distinguish between apocalyptic visions (involving the end of the world and the Last Judgment), visions of saints, accounts of imaginary journeys to regions beyond the grave and allegories concerning man's future state. Since the purpose of this study is not, primarily, to classify the representations of the happy otherworld (heaven or paradise) according to the form in which they have been cast, but to enable the reader to compare the mental pictures heaven or hell have evoked in the minds of Christian and Buddhist believers and how these have been expressed by artists and writers, no attempt will be made to adopt such a classification. On the other hand, in this particular case, it has been found necessary to separate those descriptions which appear to derive from the Book of Revelation, from those others—either composite, or referring to paradisal regions beyond the limitations and distempers of this mortal life—the setting of which is more properly terrestrial in appearance, while the degress of their bliss is far removed (quantitatively at least) from that pure intellectual love of God that is in itself the very essence of the Christian heaven.

The Apocalypse of St. John, on account of its superior authority no less than by reason of its imaginative power, has been the main source of all future (Christian) representa-

Buddhist Brahmaloka and Devaloka—which are not however eternal. (23) The last two, while frequently presenting striking analogies with the heavens as described by Dante (24), are in a sense the extension of the terrestrial universe in that form and desire still exist as well as sensual pleasures which, however, are raised to a higher power (Devaloka). But even the Buddhist higher heavens of concentration are only temporary and their inhabitants will have to be reborn as men before they can attain ultimate liberation. By insisting upon their transitoriness (25) Buddhism, both Hinayana and Mahayana, greatly diminished their importance and ranked them among the unhappy states where the possibility of hearing the Law proclaimed and so obtaining enlightenment are very remote. Mahayana, indeed, reaches a step further with the Pure Land doctrine, which may be viewed as a positive attempt to draw the faithful away from the allurements of a bliss that is only deceptive and temporary. The descriptions of such paradises, as will be seen from the examples later to be quoted, are in the main sensuous, though less so than the Pauranic ones. It is only in such later works as Asanga's *Mahayana Sutralamkara,* Asvagosha's *Awakening of Faith,* and in the poems of Santideva and of later Hindu philosophers like Ramanuja, that the conception of a perfect bliss in union with and in contemplation of Buddha is fully developed, thus giving rise to a form of mysticism which has many parallels in the West. The result of such an evolution seems to have been not a supersession of Nirvana as the ultimate goal, but a less negative and intellectual development of it, parallel to that of the Paradise idea considered either as a symbol or, like in Sukhâvatî (Amida's Paradise in the West), Abhiratî, the realm of

final resurrection, at what time the Gospel will have been spread everywhere and the Jewish Nation be regenerated, and to the Millenium proper when the present universe will be destroyed and the Last Judgment and the Resurrection of the Body will be followed by the establishment of the Heavenly Jerusalem. (20) Equally if not more frequently described, especially by Catholic writers, are the paradisal regions possibly because they lend themselves more easily to graphic treatment, and partly because of their association with the myth of the golden age which appears in many parts of the world. The belief in such a remote period of world history, when the earth was at peace, death unknown or divested of all its subsequent fears, happiness and plenty reigned, 'the lion lay down by the lamb' and man was not man's enemy, is found in Brahmanic and Buddhist cosmology as well as in that of the Semitic races (Garden of Eden) from whence it passed to Christianity, and in to Celtic, Norse and Classical mythology. This was followed by a period of degeneration in the course of which the happy age disappears. The rememberance of it, however, dies hard and is still longingly cherished. So firm and almost universally was the belief in the existence of a fragment of that blessed country in some remote corner of the world, that some indeed journeyed forth in search of it. (21) The Earthly Paradise placed by Dante on the top of the Mount of Purgatory is perhaps the most famous Christian example, while the Island of the Blest, the Paradise of Birds (Pilgrimage of St. Brendan) (22), Y-Breasil, Avalon and many others are legendary regions of the same kind. Separate from these, reserved to mortals, are the abodes of the angels, gods, immortals and a few chosen humans—Olympus, Niffleheim the Brahman and

in the pages that follow, are perhaps less illuminating on the formal side than as allowing the reader, however partially, to enter in to the spirit that informs and inspires such works that should be regarded as acts of faith, love and devotion, which soar above theology and philosophy to the realms of pure being.

\*   \*   \*   \*   \*

As regards the representations of the Abodes of the Blessed in Christianity and Buddhism, it is convenient as well as necessary to distinguish between Earthly Paradise, Paradise, and the Empyrean Heaven of Christian accounts, and between the Pure (Buddha) Lands (Paradise) and that state of inexpressible bliss outside time and space as a result of achieving the Buddha state that, according to Asanga, 'as the totality of all the ideals' includes Nirvana. (15) These distinctions cannot however be considered absolute. If the difference between Paradise and the Empyrean is clearly marked, as much cannot be said for that between Paradise and Earthly Paradise, (16) in all texts. The latter often includes many descriptive elements found in the former (17) especially as regards landscape which seems to follow the traditional descriptions of paradise (as distinct from heaven) found in the Bible (18), Oriental, Celtic, and classical legends of the 'Insulae Fortunatae'. (19) In Catholic Christianity the actual disposition of the heavens follows the classical conception of Ptolemy and the ideas of Plato and Aristotle adapted to Christian cosmological notions, under the influence of the syncretism of late Jewish beliefs containing elements from neighbouring civilizations, and of the apocalyptic visions of St. Peter and, in particular of St. John. Strictly speaking, the latter refers to the judgment and

for the Pure Land Sects) not of works, and of enlightenment. The whole doctrine of the transference of merit, which plays so vital a part in Mahyana, offers no real analogy to that of the Atonement, the very essence of which is that it alone has made it possible for man to escape from the bondage of original sin. Heaven, eternal blessedness, salvation, were closed to all but those few who were directly translated to the celestial regions, until the coming of Christ, as dramatically illustrated in the Gospel of Nicodemus and in the episode of the Harrowing of Hell that has been so frequently treated by Christian writers and artists. But Nirvana could be attained by mankind independently of the Buddha who, however, pointed out a new way to it. *Bhakti* (devotion) for the Mahayanist becomes an increasingly important element in salvation, but ultimate liberation, whether in this or other states where it is possible, or in the Western Paradise of Amida, demands as its prerequisite that the conception of death and life as realities should be discarded completely, since they are the main obstacles to the realization of the supreme truth of being —that all empyrical reality, viewed transcendentally, is an illusion (*Maya*), and that transcendental reality (*Nirvana*) is beyond form and beyond change. (14) It is the understanding of this which, alone, makes liberation and perfect freedom possible. Whether for the average Christian or the Buddhist, philosophical or mystical ideas are meaningless because unthinkable, they are none the less the very breath and life of the religion they profess and colour their beliefs even if they are unaware of it, just as they inevitably colour all representations of the after-life. The differences and even the similarities that will be found between the various examples of paradise quoted

with Nirvana, and implies complete and final liberation from the continuous stream of actual lives (*samsara*) and the cessation of birth and death. (13)

It should further be noted in passing, that the conception and representation of future blessedness no less than its ultimate significance is necessarily affected by the wide differences that exist between Buddhists and Christians as regards the essence and meaning of Salvation. For the Buddhist salvation does not imply as for the Christian, escape from eternal death and damnation due to Original Sin, but primarily from an eternity of successive lives, even if such an eternity of life is caused by error and ignorance leading to sin. Christ's promise to the thief on the cross—'today thou shalt be with me in paradise'—is a message of hope such as was never given by Amida, nor could indeed have been given. What Amida's vow carried with it was the promise that, by viritue of it, believers at the hour of death might rest assured of being saved immediately from the results of their evil actions and from unending life, and be granted admission to his paradise. There seems no reason to conclude, however, that this was the only means of achieving ultimate salvation. Although it was an easier and perhaps safer one, there were other roads to salvation and Nirvana, but immeasurably longer and almost impossibly difficult. All men being potentially Buddhas, and Buddha himself being a very man, and not *ex aeterno* divine, salvation became possible for all, provided that certain prescriptions were fulfilled. That all disabilities and sins could, according to the Amidist view, be overridden as it were through the power of the Vow, did not substantially alter the situation. Salvation is ultimately a question of faith (at least

therefore, in my opinion, as mere superstitious practices. Making all necessary allowances for intrinsic divergences, the same holds good for similar Christian acts of devotion.

In using the term 'otherworld' it is well to keep in mind the profound difference existing between the Buddhist and the Christian conception of it. Whereas in the latter it signifies a non-material existence beyond death, in the former it involves a renewed life upon earth which, although classified (under normal conditions) as one of the unfortunate states, is nevertheless superior even to a temporary sojourn, however extended, in one of the heavens. All such phases of the afterlife, according to Mrs Rhys Davids, are more properly, *anchistological* rather than *eschatological,* being concerned with proximate rather than ultimate things. In this sense Purgatory belongs to anchistology, with this important qualification, that it is but another different, stage of human existence, one of the many possible categories of sentiency into which a man may be reborn after death, such as is the case with the regions of hell or the realm of hungry ghosts in Buddhism. (12) For the Buddhist the ultimate phase which is properly the subject of eschatology, may only be reached when the karma-seed has become exhausted, not merely when the thread of mortality has been cut, as in Christianity. It is only then that man enters upon the way that has no return, i.e. the path to final Nirvana. The conception of the Pure Lands of the Buddhas found in Mahayana Buddhism is anchistological in so far it refers to a state that may be achieved immediately after death and is closer therefore in this respect to the Christian one of Paradise, but at the same time eschatological since, potentially if not actually, it is concerned

> La charactéristique d'une image est son aptitude à promouvior la mèditation et le yoga. L'artisan humain doit être donc méditatif. En dehors de la méditation il n'y a pas autre moyen de connaître le charactère d'une image; l'observation directe est incomplète....Peinture, sculpture ou poème sont oeuvres pies avant de passer pour oeuvres belles—c'est l'opération guidée par une pure pensée chez le peintre, le sculpteur ou le poéte et chez celui pour qui l'artiste a travaillé. Mais l'oeuvre c'est un intermediaire, un moyen fragile et imparfait...L'art instaure, pour ainsi dire, une *paraphysique,* distincte de la métaphysique.
> Il ne nous delivre pas, mais nous 'divertit' au sens étymologique et pascalien du mot. (8)

The numberless works of all kinds directly or indirectly concerned with the hereafter Buddhist or Christian, are eloquent witnesses to the universality and persistence of a belief in an otherworld which in some measure will redress the balance of good and evil in this, but even more they serve to crystallize and to give concrete form to innermost convictions based upon a 'lay philosophy of things' (9) which religion confirms, expands and systematizes. Such representations are to be regarded less as acceptance of a dogma, than as active belief in the Truth which will make one whole—in other words they are an act of faith on the part of the artist which gives rise to and expresses a corresponding act on the part of the believer. The references to the importance of making copies of such sutras as the *Lotus* (10) and the orders issued at frequent intervals in the VIIth, VIIIth and later centuries, to have copies made of certain Buddhist paintings (11) in Japan, are evidence of what has just been said and cannot be viewed

itself a form of aesthetic as well as of dogmatic expression. The relegation of religious art to a special (often inferior) category, as well as its gradual separation from everyday life, has never been pushed to extremes. In the case of Japan it is only perhaps in works of purely Western inspiration —imitative rather than creative—(5) that the religious-philosophical element which seems to be inextricably woven into the Japanese aesthetic consciousness, is sometimes deliberately ignored. Nor is this contradicted by the well-known fact that from the XVth century onwards art may be seen to concern itself with the representation of secular subjects, as in the case of the secularization of Zen painting described by Anezaki, particularly during the Genroku period. (6) The spirit which inspired such painting as well as poetry combined a 'calm enjoyment or humorous observation of life and nature even in the midst of a busy life', achieving a happy blend of 'reality' and 'vacuity' that, as taught by Bashô, consisted in 'living a life unfettered and soaring, never bewildered by the vicissitudes of life, never disturbed by gain or loss'. Graces, delicacy, and serenity, these are the three requisites for realising the middle path between reality and vacuity. Such an attitude, if apparently far removed from the mysticism of the Amidist, was none the less the outcome of one and the same religious belief in the unity of all creation interpenetrated with and expressive of the universal Buddha nature. (7)

M. P. Masson Oursel discussing Indian Aesthetics drew attention to the important fact that for the Indians—and this is in a large measure applicable to the Japanese and Chinese artist—

the modern approach to the *Apocalypse*, the vision of Ezeckiel and of other Hebrew prophets, that are praised as fine examples of Jewish poetry but above all for the beauty of the translation. (3)

While no one would deny that it is possible to appreciate such works purely from the aesthetic point of view, it must also be evident that the horizons descried from such a vantage point are somewhat limited. As an eminent Scottish professor recently expressed it:—

> Literature and music and all the arts, the love of nature, science and philosophy—these must be granted a radical independence of a certain kind within their own spheres, yet such independence cannot be regarded as the ultimate fact in the case. The true end of their being has not been attained when they have pushed to the limit their own departmental curiosity, but only when they have 'brought in their sheaves' to the harvest of a riper wisdom and a profounder love..The greatest art of all has been produced within the framework of a definite otherworldly outlook. It is as if the beauties of eternity had proved, even when judged by purely aesthetic standards, to be the greatest beauties of all. There is no other beauty like unto the Beauty of Holiness. Could Gothic architecture, could the *Divina Comedia,* could the prose of the Authorized Version conceivably have come into being for their own sakes or of their own momentum alone—as mere masterpieces of decorative loveliness? (4)

For East Asia, however, no such an apology is required. In India, as in Japan, no hard and fast distinction between religious and secular art seems to exist, since all art is ultimately and in a wide sense religious and, conversely, religion is

in 'the evidence of things not seen' is considered irrelevant or at best subsidiary to it whereas, in reality, it is its only basis and justification. Consequently the evaluation of eschatological works by aesthetic standards alone is, of necessity, inadequate and incomplete. The attempt to isolate as it were the artistic side, in other words to accept these eschatological representations as works of art, while at the same time denying validity to the beliefs of which they are the expression, on the grounds that they are nothing more than naive, confused, and frequently ridiculous superstitions of a barbarous and unenlightened age, philosophically unsound and, from a religious viewpoint, even inconsistent with the character and original teachings of the founders of Christianity or Buddhism, and possess, at best, only an ethnological interest—obscures their true significance and empties them of all life. If a somewhat trivial analogy may be conceded, one might as reasonably insist that the Witches and the Ghost are not essential to *Macbeth* and *Hamlet,* and that those plays would be in no way substantially altered if the Thane of Cawdor and the Prince of Denmark had not believed in them or, venturing a step further, that Shakespeare merely considered them as stage devices having a popular appeal.

In the case of Dante, Giotto, Fra Angelico as of many anonymous Christian and Buddhist writers and painters who have described states of blessedness or damnation, it is frequently asserted that where they have achieved greatness, it has been in spite rather than by reason of the alleged limitations imposed upon them by the dogmas and traditions which, in reality, have made them what they are. The attempt to separate content from form has been even more evident in

Paradoxical though the statement may seem, it is with Christianity—and to a much lesser degree with Mahayana Buddhism—that Hell (or other states in which human beings pay the price of their wrong-doing) attains its full spiritual significance and grandeur, and ceases to be merely the transference of a man-made plan of retribution to the world beyond this.

(2) In approaching eschatological works whether of 'licensed imagination' or of 'dogmatic revelation'—visions, apocalypses, journeys to the otherworld and descriptions of regions of blessedness or torment outside or within the terrestrial sphere, whatsoever the medium used by the author, which derive inspiration from a belief in a future state, no proper understanding or appreciation seems possible unless the reality as well as the truth of such beliefs is frankly recognized without reservations or concessions to the ignorance or naivete of our ancestors. Whatever our own opinions and beliefs may be, we must first accept those beliefs as possessing vital significance and as being the source from which the writer receives the inspiration to create. The theory of the absolute autonomy of art, important as it undeniably is in certain cases, is here liable to lead to misinterpretation and errors in judgment when applied too rigidly. Thus, frequently, professional critics in the West—and sometimes, though to a far lesser degree in the East, at least in Buddhist countries—have denied any purposiveness or justification to religious art other than the expression of an individual aesthetic activity. Religious art, as such, stands condemned by them in so far as its primary aim is to illustrate dogmatic truths or convey transcendental religious beliefs, because faith in 'the substance of things hoped for' and

feel to be of great importance for the proper understanding of the development of eschatological ideas in relation to the spiritual history of the West and of Eastern Asia.

It had been originally intended to deal also with the purgatorial regions and hell, but for reasons of length as well as of system, it has seemed preferable to treat the subject separately in another essay, in relation to the closely connected questions of Sin, Retribution, Punishment and the experience of Death. There seems, moreover to be some reason for believing that the conception of hell in general and its elaborate differentiation, is somewhat later than that of heaven, and is conditioned by elements which are, originally at least, less religious than ethical, and connected with the social evolution of the peoples under consideration.

The conception of paradise or heaven or, generally speaking, of a state of ultimate bliss, appears to have spontaneously arisen as the result of a natural desire to find some satisfactory explanation of the mystery of life and death and as an aspiration towards a superior form of existence, the value of which is enhanced by comparison with the evils of life upon earth and even more by reference to future punishments attending wrongdoers in this life. One might also suggest that the fear of the latter could act as a positive incentive to the achievement of paradise, in proportion as ultimate blessedness (or salvation) through the merits of Christ's sacrifice on the Cross and of Buddha's great vow, became less fortuitous or depended mainly upon conscious human effort. Christianity, no less than Amida-Buddhism profoundly affected the whole conception of the future of man and gave a powerful impulse to the definition and spiritualization of the idea of absolute blessedness.

# CHRISTIAN AND BUDDHIST REPRESENTATIONS OF THE HAPPY OTHERWORLD

....the essential Beauty of Holiness,
pass'd her creativ joy into the creature's heart,
to take back from his and her Adoration robes
and royal crown of his Imagination and Love.
          Bridges, Testament of Beauty, I, 622-25

In a previous essay (1) I attempted to outline in a summary fashion what, to me, appeared to be some of the fundamental differences between the religious experience of the Buddhist East and the Catholic West, as expressed in their respective conceptions of the Otherworld.

In the present paper, I propose to deal with what, in general terms, may best be described as the Abodes of the Blessed—i.e. Paradise and Heaven. With this end in view I have selected and quoted from a number of Christian and Buddhist texts, canonical and otherwise, which serve to show how artists and writers conceived and represented such paradisiac regions adding at the end, by way of further illustration, a few plates reproducing Buddhist and Christian paintings which further confirm the interdependence between the texts and the pictorial representations of paradise. In both cases the selection has had to be restricted, especially as regards the pictorial side, since to do even partial justice to the latter would require special treatment in a separate volume. It is hoped, however, that the illustrations will prove of some interest and prepare the way for an exhaustive study of a subject which I

# CHRISTIAN AND BUDDHIST REPRESENTATIONS OF THE HAPPY OTHERWORLD

> ....the essential Beauty of Holiness,
> pass'd her creativ joy into the creature's heart,
> to take back from his and her Adoration robes
> and royal crown of his Imagination and Love.
>       Bridges, Testament of Beauty, I, 622-25

In a previous essay (1) I attempted to outline in a summary fashion what, to me, appeared to be some of the fundamental differences between the religious experience of the Buddhist East and the Catholic West, as expressed in their respective conceptions of the Otherworld.

In the present paper, I propose to deal with what, in general terms, may best be described as the Abodes of the Blessed— i.e. Paradise and Heaven. With this end in view I have selected and quoted from a number of Christian and Buddhist texts, canonical and otherwise, which serve to show how artists and writers conceived and represented such paradisiac regions adding at the end, by way of further illustration, a few plates reproducing Buddhist and Christian paintings which further confirm the interdependence between the texts and the pictorial representations of paradise. In both cases the selection has had to be restricted, especially as regards the pictorial side, since to do even partial justice to the latter would require special treatment in a separate volume. It is hoped, however, that the illustrations will prove of some interest and prepare the way for an exhaustive study of a subject which I

# CHRISTIAN AND BUDDHIST REPRESENTATIONS OF THE HAPPY OTHERWORLD

by

ARUNDELL DEL RE

Annual Bulletin
of
The Department of Literature

# GENGO TO BUNGAKU

Vol. IV

---

Published
by
The Faculty of Literature and Politics
Taihoku Imperial University
Taiwan, Japan
1940

Annual Bulletin
of
The Department of Literature

# GENGO TO BUNGAKU

(Language and Literature)

Vol. IV.

## CHRISTIAN AND BUDDHIST REPRESENTATIONS OF THE HAPPY OTHERWORLD

by

ARUNDELL DEL RE

Published
by
The Faculty of Literature and Politics
Taihoku Imperial University
Taiwan, Japan
1940